RESTORATIVE JUSTICE CIRCLES

Healing Through Community Support

WORKBOOK

SECOND EDITION

DR. MAXWELL SHIMBA

Published in Manhattan, New York by Shimba Publishing, LLC.

Shimba Publishing LLC

Table of Contents

RESTORATIVE JUSTICE CIRCLES – WORKBOOK

RESTORATIVE JUSTICE CIRCLES – WORKBOOK

Healing Through Community Support

Second Edition

Dr. Maxwell Shimba

How to Use This Workbook

This workbook is designed to be used alongside *Restorative Justice Circles (Second Edition)* or as a standalone training manual for individuals, study groups, facilitator training programs, and community circles.

Each chapter includes:

- **Learning Objectives** – Clear goals for your study
- **Key Concepts** – Condensed principles from the book
- **Reflection Questions** – Personal and group journaling prompts
- **Group Exercises & Circle Practices** – Experiential learning activities
- **Case Analysis** – Real-world applications to examine
- **Practical Assignments** – Action steps for implementation
- **Facilitator Notes** – Guidance for leading group sessions

WORKBOOK INTRODUCTION

Personal Commitment Statement

Before beginning your journey through restorative justice, pause to center yourself. This work is not merely academic—it is transformative. It will challenge your assumptions about justice, harm, accountability, and healing.

Write a brief statement answering:

- **Why do I want to learn restorative justice?**
- **What injustices or conflicts have shaped my understanding of justice?**
- **Am I willing to be transformed—not just informed—by this process?**

My Commitment Statement:

Learning Objectives for the Introduction

By completing this introductory section, you will be able to:

1. **Define restorative justice** and distinguish it from retributive justice
2. **Identify the six key elements** of restorative justice circles
3. **Explain the theological, philosophical, and psychological foundations** of restorative practice
4. **Articulate the concept of restorative cycles** and their connection to biological and social healing
5. **Describe the structure and purpose** of the fifteen chapters in this book

Key Concepts from Chapter 1

1. Restorative Justice Defined

Restorative justice is a paradigm shift from retributive justice. While retributive justice asks:

- What law was broken?

- Who broke it?
- What punishment do they deserve?

Restorative justice asks:

- Who has been harmed?
- What are their needs?
- Whose obligations are these?
- How can harm be repaired?

2. The Jurisprudential Shift

For over eight centuries, Western legal systems have defined crime as an offense against the state, displacing victims from the justice process. Restorative justice restores victims, offenders, and communities as active participants in pursuing justice.

3. Theological Foundation

The modern restorative justice movement emerged from Christian (particularly Mennonite) soil. Key biblical themes include:

- God's justice as primarily restorative, not retributive
- The image of God (*imago Dei*) in every person
- The ministry of reconciliation (2 Corinthians 5:18-19)
- Jubilee restoration (Leviticus 25)

4. Philosophical Anthropology of the Circle

The circle embodies radical equality. Unlike hierarchical courtrooms, the circle arrangement communicates:

- Every person possesses inherent dignity
- Every perspective is necessary for full understanding

- Wisdom resides in the assembled community, not experts alone

5. Six Key Elements of Restorative Justice Circles

Element	Meaning
Inclusivity	All affected parties participate
Voluntariness	No coercion; free consent required
Respect and Equality	Every voice carries equal value
Accountability	Active responsibility, not passive punishment
Reparation	Tangible actions to repair harm
Reintegration	Restoration to full community membership

6. Restorative Cycles

Restorative cycles are the inherent, self-organizing processes by which living systems recover from injury. Examples include:

- Cellular autophagy and tissue regeneration
- Circadian rhythms of rest and activity
- Wound healing (inflammation → proliferation → remodeling)
- Ecological succession after disturbance

Restorative justice circles are liturgical enactments of these cycles—creating sacred time and space for healing to occur.

7. The Interdisciplinary Nature of Restorative Justice

This book integrates:

- **Theology** – Divine mandate for reconciliation
- **Law** – Jurisprudential frameworks and human rights
- **Psychology** – Trauma recovery, empathy development
- **Philosophy** – Moral imagination, equity, practical wisdom
- **Biology** – Restorative cycles in nature

8. Chapter Overview

The book is organized into fifteen chapters covering principles, history, implementation, facilitator roles, circle process, case studies, challenges, psychological impact, and applications in schools, workplaces, criminal justice, and global contexts.

Reflection Questions

Take time to write or discuss these questions. Allow them to surface your own experiences, assumptions, and hopes.

1. **Personal Experience with Justice**

- When have you experienced justice that felt truly healing?
- When have you experienced justice that felt harmful or inadequate?
- What made the difference?

2. **Understanding of Crime and Harm**
    - Before reading this introduction, how did you define "justice"?
    - How does the restorative question—"Who has been harmed?"—change your perspective on a conflict you've experienced or witnessed?

3. **Theological or Philosophical Grounding**
    - If you come from a faith tradition, what resources does your tradition offer for understanding restoration?
    - If you do not identify with a faith tradition, what philosophical or ethical commitments draw you to restorative justice?

4. **Restorative Cycles in Your Life**
    - Can you identify natural cycles of wounding and healing in your own life or community?
    - What conditions helped healing occur? What conditions hindered it?

5. **Personal Readiness**
    - This work requires "transformed hearts—people who have themselves received mercy and therefore can extend it." (p. 7)
    - Where have you received mercy? How might that experience equip you for restorative work?
    - What fears or hesitations do you bring to this study?

Group Exercise: Talking Circle on "What Justice Means to Me"

Purpose: To experience the circle process while exploring personal understandings of justice.

Time: 45–60 minutes

Materials: A talking piece (any object with meaning—stone, feather, carved wood, etc.), comfortable seating in a circle

Facilitator Instructions:

1. **Opening (5 minutes)**
    - Welcome participants and explain the purpose: "We will experience a simplified restorative circle to explore our personal understandings of justice."
    - Introduce the talking piece: "Only the person holding this object may speak. All others listen without interrupting. You may pass if you wish."
    - Establish confidentiality: "What is shared in this circle stays in this circle."
2. **Check-In Round (10 minutes)**
    - Pass the talking piece. Each person shares their name and one word describing how they are arriving today.
3. **Sharing Round (20 minutes)**
    - Pass the talking piece. Each person responds to the prompt: "Share a story or experience that has shaped your understanding of justice—whether from personal life, something you've witnessed, or something you've studied."
    - Allow silence between speakers. No cross-talk or response.
4. **Reflection Round (10 minutes)**
    - Pass the talking piece. Each person shares: "What are you taking away from hearing others' stories?"
5. **Closing (5 minutes)**
    - Facilitator offers brief summary of themes heard.
    - Thank participants for their honesty and vulnerability.

  - Close with a moment of silence or simple words: "This circle is now closed. Thank you for being present."

Facilitator Notes:

- Model respectful listening throughout.
- If someone becomes emotional, allow silence; offer validation without rushing to "fix."
- After the circle, debrief the *process* as well as the *content*: How did it feel to speak with the talking piece? To listen without interrupting? To be in a circle rather than rows?

Case Analysis: The Theology of Restorative Justice

Read the following excerpt from Chapter 1 (pages 5-7) carefully:

"The modern restorative justice movement, perhaps one of the most significant social movements of our time, was born in a Christian home to Christian parents... The Scriptures present a God whose justice is not primarily retributive but restorative—a God who does not merely punish transgression but actively works to reconcile all things to Himself... The Jubilee year (Leviticus 25) was a systemic restorative intervention: debts forgiven, land returned, slaves liberated, families reunited. This was not charity but justice—structural restoration designed to prevent the permanent stratification of society... When we sit in a circle to listen to a victim's pain, when we create space for an offender's accountability, when we labor together for reparation and

reintegration, we are doing nothing less than joining God in the work of reconciliation."

Questions for Analysis:

1. **Biblical Foundations:**
    - What specific biblical texts and themes does the author identify as foundational to restorative justice?
    - How does the author distinguish restorative justice from "charity"?

2. **Theological Claims:**
    - The author claims restorative justice is "not merely a program but a reflection of the divine order inscribed upon the human heart." What evidence or arguments support this claim?
    - What does it mean to say restorative justice is "spirituality" rather than "technique"?

3. **Implications for Practice:**
    - If restorative justice is participation in divine reconciliation, how might this affect:
        - The way facilitators prepare for circles?
        - The way participants are treated?
        - The expectations for outcomes?

4. **Personal Response:**
    - How does this theological framing resonate with or challenge your own worldview?
    - Regardless of your religious background, what might it mean to approach restorative work as "vocation" rather than "technique"?

Practical Assignment: Observing Justice

Assignment: Between now and your next session, observe how justice (or its absence) operates in your everyday environment.

Instructions:

1. **Notice** – Pay attention to:
    - How conflicts are handled in your workplace, family, or community
    - News stories about crime and punishment
    - Conversations about fairness, accountability, and harm
    - Your own internal responses when you are wronged or when you wrong another
2. **Journal** – Record at least three observations using this framework:
    - What happened? (Describe the situation briefly)
    - How was it addressed? (What process or response occurred?)
    - Was the response primarily retributive or restorative? (Why do you think so?)
    - What needs were left unaddressed? What needs were met?
3. **Reflect** – Write one paragraph: How did this observation deepen or challenge your understanding of restorative justice?

Observation 1:

Observation 2:

Observation 3:

Reflection Paragraph:

Facilitator Notes for the Introduction

Before the Session:

1. **Read Chapter 1 thoroughly.** Familiarize yourself with the key concepts, especially the six elements of restorative justice circles and the concept of restorative cycles.
2. **Prepare the space.** Arrange chairs in a circle. Have talking pieces available. Create a welcoming, safe atmosphere.
3. **Know your participants.** If this is a group, be aware of any recent conflicts or traumas that might affect participation. Consider meeting individually with anyone who might need additional support.
4. **Gather materials.** Have copies of this workbook, pens, and any handouts ready.

During the Session:

1. **Opening (10 minutes)**
    - Welcome participants warmly.
    - Review the "How to Use This Workbook" section.
    - Explain that this journey will involve both learning and personal transformation.

2. **Introductions (10 minutes)**
    - If this is a group, have each person share their name and one hope for this study.
3. **Key Concepts Review (20 minutes)**
    - Briefly present the key concepts from the introduction.
    - Focus on the six elements and restorative cycles.
    - Invite questions and clarification.
4. **Circle Exercise (45–60 minutes)**
    - Conduct the talking circle on "What Justice Means to Me."
    - Allow adequate time; don't rush.
5. **Debrief (15 minutes)**
    - After the circle, discuss the *process*: How did it feel? What was challenging? What was surprising?
    - Connect participants' experiences to the six elements of restorative justice circles.
6. **Case Analysis Discussion (20 minutes)**
    - If time permits, discuss the theological case analysis as a group.
    - Allow diverse perspectives; there is no single "right" answer.
7. **Assignments (5 minutes)**
    - Review the practical assignment.
    - Encourage participants to keep a journal throughout the study.
8. **Closing (5 minutes)**
    - Thank participants.

  - Preview the next chapter (Principles of Restorative Justice Circles).
  - Close with a moment of silence or a brief reading (e.g., Psalm 23, a quote from the book, or a simple blessing).

After the Session:

- Reflect on what went well and what could be improved.
- Follow up with any participants who seemed distressed.
- Prepare for Chapter 2.

Key Teaching Points to Emphasize:

- Restorative justice is a **paradigm shift**, not just a new technique.
- The **six elements** are interdependent—each requires the others.
- **Restorative cycles** connect restorative justice to natural, biological, and spiritual processes.
- This work requires **personal transformation**, not just information acquisition.
- The **circle itself** embodies the values of equality, respect, and shared wisdom.

Personal Journal: Introduction

Use this space for ongoing reflections throughout your study.

Date: _______________

What I'm learning:

What I'm questioning:

What I'm feeling:

How this connects to my life/work:

A question I want to explore further:

"The restorative cycles of creation await our participation. The God of reconciliation calls us to join the divine work of making all things new." — Dr. Maxwell Shimba

CHAPTER 01

Introduction to Restorative Justice

Learning Objectives

By completing this chapter, you will be able to:

- **Understand the difference** between retributive and restorative justice
- **Identify how harm affects** victims, offenders, and communities
- **Articulate a restorative definition** of justice
- **Recognize the shift** from state-centered to community-centered justice
- **Connect restorative justice** to theological, philosophical, and psychological foundations

Key Concepts

1. Crime as Harm to Relationships

In the retributive paradigm, crime is defined as a violation of the state—a broken law requiring punishment. In the restorative paradigm, crime is understood as harm to people and relationships. This shift has profound implications:

Retributive View	Restorative View
Crime violates the state	Crime harms victims, offenders, and communities
Justice requires punishment	Justice requires repair
Offender is passive recipient of sanctions	Offender is active participant in accountability
Victim is evidence	Victim is a stakeholder
Community is spectator	Community is participant

2. Justice as Healing and Repair

Restorative justice seeks not merely to balance suffering with suffering but to restore what has been broken. This includes:

- **Material repair** – Returning stolen property, paying restitution, repairing damage
- **Emotional healing** – Acknowledging pain, validating victims' experiences, addressing trauma
- **Relational restoration** – Rebuilding trust, repairing damaged relationships
- **Community reconciliation** – Strengthening the social fabric torn by harm

Justice, in this view, is measured not by how much punishment was inflicted but by how much healing occurred.

3. Community as a Stakeholder

Conventional justice systems exclude communities, treating crime as a matter between the state and the offender. Restorative justice recognizes that:

- Communities are **harmed** by crime (loss of safety, trust, cohesion)
- Communities have **resources** for healing (relationships, knowledge, support)
- Communities have **responsibilities** (to support victims, to hold offenders accountable, to address underlying conditions)
- Communities must be **involved** in creating solutions

4. The Paradigm Shift

Howard Zehr, often called the "grandfather of restorative justice," articulated the paradigm shift through contrasting questions:

Retributive Questions	Restorative Questions
What law was broken?	Who has been harmed?
Who broke it?	What are their needs?
What punishment do they deserve?	Whose obligations are these?
	How can harm be repaired?

5. The Three Stakeholders

Restorative justice recognizes three primary stakeholders in any harm:

- **Victims** – Those directly harmed, who need acknowledgment, validation, safety, and reparation
- **Offenders** – Those who caused harm, who need accountability, support for change, and opportunity to make amends
- **Communities** – Those affected by the ripple effects of harm, who need restoration of trust and safety

6. The Injustice Gap

Research by Witvliet and colleagues demonstrates that victims experience an "injustice gap"—the discrepancy between their desired resolution and the actual outcome. This gap generates chronic stress, dysregulates the autonomic nervous system, and contributes over time to disease. Restorative justice narrows this gap by providing:

- Acknowledgment of harm
- Accountability from offenders
- Opportunity for voice and participation
- Tangible reparation

7. Theological and Philosophical Foundations

The modern restorative justice movement emerged from Christian (particularly Mennonite) soil but has been embraced across faith traditions and secular contexts. Key foundations include:

- **The imago Dei** – Every person bears God's image and possesses inherent dignity
- **Shalom** – Comprehensive well-being through right relationship
- **Jubilee** – Systemic restoration of relationships and resources
- **Covenant** – Faithful commitment to relationship beyond contract
- **Ubuntu** – "A person is a person through persons" (African philosophy)

Reflection Questions

Take time to write or discuss these questions. Allow them to surface your own experiences, assumptions, and hopes.

1. How were conflicts handled in your family or community growing up?

Think back to your earliest experiences with conflict, wrongdoing, and justice. What messages did you receive—explicitly or implicitly—about how to respond when harm occurred?

2. What emotions arise when you hear the word "justice"?

Notice your emotional response. Does "justice" evoke hope? Fear? Anger? Satisfaction? Cynicism? Where do these emotions come from?

3. Have you ever felt punished but not healed? Explain.

Describe an experience where consequences were imposed but you did not feel made whole—whether as someone who caused harm, someone who was harmed, or someone who witnessed harm.

4. Who was affected by a conflict you've experienced?

Think of a specific conflict or harm from your life. List all the people who were affected—directly and indirectly. How far does the ripple effect extend?

5. What did you need that you didn't receive?

In that same conflict, what did you need that you didn't get? What would have helped you heal?

6. How might your life be different if justice had focused on healing rather than punishment?

Imagine an alternative response to that conflict. How might your relationships, your sense of safety, your trust in others, or your view of yourself be different?

Exercise 1: Justice Comparison Table

Purpose: To clarify the differences between retributive and restorative justice by applying both frameworks to a concrete situation.

Instructions: Consider a specific harm—either one you have experienced, witnessed, or learned about. Complete the table below, describing how retributive justice and restorative justice would each approach this situation.

Choose a harm to analyze:

Element	Retributive Approach	Restorative Approach
How is the harm defined? (What makes it wrong?)		
Who are the stakeholders? (Who has a stake in resolution?)		
What questions are asked?		
What process is used?		
What is the role of the victim?		
What is the role of the offender?		
What is the role of the community?		
What outcome is sought?		

Element	Retributive Approach	Restorative Approach
How is success measured?		

Reflection: After completing the table, write two paragraphs comparing the approaches. What does each framework reveal? What does each obscure? Which approach better addresses the needs you identified earlier?

Exercise 2: Identifying Stakeholders

Purpose: To practice identifying all those affected by harm, moving beyond the obvious direct victim and offender.

Scenario:

*A 15-year-old student, Marcus, has been bullying a classmate, Elena, for several months. The bullying includes mocking her appearance, excluding her from group activities, and spreading rumors on social media. Last week, the bullying escalated to physical intimidation in the hallway. Elena has missed several days of school due to anxiety. Marcus has been suspended multiple times but the behavior continues.

Instructions: List every person or group who has been affected by this situation. For each stakeholder, identify:

- How they have been harmed
- What they might need for healing

Stakeholder	Nature of Harm	Needs for Healing
Elena (victim)		
Marcus (offender)		

Stakeholder	Nature of Harm	Needs for Healing

Add as many rows as you need.

Discussion Questions:

- Were you surprised by how many stakeholders you identified?
- Which stakeholders are typically ignored in conventional disciplinary responses?
- How might the needs of different stakeholders conflict? How might they align?
- What would a truly restorative response to this situation include?

Exercise 3: The Injustice Gap

Purpose: To understand the psychological concept of the "injustice gap" through personal experience.

Background: Research by Charlotte vanOyen Witvliet demonstrates that when victims experience an "injustice gap"—the discrepancy between their desired resolution and the actual outcome—they experience chronic stress, dysregulated autonomic nervous systems, and negative health outcomes. Restorative justice narrows this gap through acknowledgment, accountability, and reparation.

Instructions:

1. Think of a time when you experienced harm that was not adequately addressed.
2. Describe the harm briefly:

   ---

3. Describe how it was addressed (or not addressed):

   ---

4. What did you need that you did not receive?

   ---

5. What would have narrowed the "injustice gap" for you?

6. How did the unresolved gap affect you—emotionally, physically, relationally?

7. If you could design a restorative response to that situation now, what would it include?

Circle Practice: "When I Was Not Heard"

Purpose: To experience the healing power of being heard and to practice circle protocol with a vulnerable prompt.

Time: 45–60 minutes

Materials: Talking piece, comfortable seating in a circle

Facilitator Instructions:

Preparation (before the circle):

- Arrange chairs in a circle with no tables or obstructions.
- Place the talking piece in the center.
- Remind participants of confidentiality: "What is shared in this circle stays in this circle."
- Acknowledge that this prompt may evoke strong emotions. Ensure support is available if needed.

Opening (5 minutes):

- Welcome participants and explain the purpose: "We will practice being in circle together, using the prompt: 'Describe a moment when you were harmed and never truly heard.'"
- Introduce or reintroduce the talking piece: "Only the person holding this object may speak. All others listen without interrupting. You may pass if you wish. There is no requirement to share."
- Review any additional ground rules (respect, confidentiality, speaking from experience).

Check-In Round (10 minutes):

- Pass the talking piece. Each person shares their name and one word describing how they are arriving today.

Sharing Round (20–30 minutes):

- Pass the talking piece. Each person who wishes responds to the prompt: "Describe a moment when you were harmed and never truly heard."
- Allow silence between speakers. Do not rush.

- If someone becomes emotional, allow silence. The facilitator may offer a brief validation ("Thank you for your courage") but should not interrupt the flow.

Reflection Round (10 minutes):

- Pass the talking piece. Each person shares: "What was it like to share or to listen?"

Closing (5 minutes):

- Facilitator offers brief summary of themes heard (without naming individuals).
- Thank participants for their honesty and vulnerability.
- Close with a moment of silence or simple words: "This circle is now closed. Thank you for being present."

After the Circle:

- Check in privately with anyone who seemed distressed.
- Reflect on the experience in your journal.

Facilitator Notes:

- This is a vulnerable prompt. Ensure you have created adequate safety through preparation and ground rules.
- Model attentive listening throughout.
- If someone becomes overwhelmed, you may offer a break or check in with them privately after.
- After the circle, you might invite brief written reflection to help participants process.

Case Study: The Kitchener Experiment (1974)

Background:

In 1974, in Kitchener, Ontario, two young men went on a vandalism spree, damaging twenty-two properties. They were ordered by a probation officer and judge to meet with their victims and make restitution. The Mennonite Central Committee facilitated these meetings—the first Victim-Offender Reconciliation Program (VORP).

This experiment is widely recognized as the beginning of the modern restorative justice movement.

What Happened:

- The offenders met face-to-face with their victims
- Victims described how the vandalism had affected them
- Offenders listened and responded
- Agreements were reached for restitution
- Both victims and offenders reported satisfaction with the process

Significance:

This experiment demonstrated that:

- Victims wanted more than punishment of offenders
- Offenders could be genuinely accountable when confronted with human impact
- Communities could play a role in justice
- A different kind of justice was possible

Questions for Analysis:

1. What made this experiment different from conventional justice?

2. Why do you think victims were satisfied with meeting the offenders, rather than simply seeing them punished?

3. What conditions made this experiment possible?

4. The Mennonite Central Committee's involvement was rooted in Anabaptist theology. How might faith commitments have shaped this experiment?

5. What lessons from this 1974 experiment remain relevant today?

Assignment: Reflective Essay

Prompt:

Write a 1–2 page reflection answering:

"Why can punishment alone not restore what harm destroys?"

Guidelines:

- Draw on the key concepts from this chapter (harm as relational, the injustice gap, stakeholder needs, restorative cycles)
- Include at least one personal observation or experience
- Reference the Kitchener case study or another example
- Consider the theological/philosophical foundations (if relevant to you)
- Conclude with implications for how you might approach conflict differently

Structure Suggestion:

- **Introduction** – State your thesis: what punishment can and cannot accomplish
- **Body Paragraph 1** – Explain what harm destroys (safety, trust, dignity, relationship)
- **Body Paragraph 2** – Explain what punishment does (and does not do) in response

- **Body Paragraph 3** – Illustrate with an example (personal, historical, or case study)
- **Body Paragraph 4** – Describe what restoration requires beyond punishment
- **Conclusion** – Summarize and connect to your own learning or practice

Reflection Space (Notes and Outline):

Personal Journal: Chapter 1

Use this space for ongoing reflections throughout your study of this chapter.

Date: ______________

Key insights I'm taking from this chapter:

Questions I still have:

How this connects to my life/work:

Emotions this chapter evoked:

One thing I want to explore further:

A commitment I'm making based on this chapter:

Facilitator Notes for Chapter 1

Before the Session:

1. **Read Chapter 1 of the main text thoroughly.** Familiarize yourself with the key concepts, especially the paradigm shift and the six key elements introduced in the Introduction (which this chapter draws from).
2. **Prepare for emotional vulnerability.** The circle practice ("When I Was Not Heard") invites participants into vulnerable territory. Ensure you have:
    - Established clear confidentiality guidelines
    - Identified support resources (counseling, trusted individuals)
    - Prepared to check in privately with anyone who becomes distressed
3. **Gather materials:**
    - Talking piece
    - Copies of this workbook for all participants
    - Whiteboard or flip chart for capturing key concepts
    - Pens or pencils
4. **Arrange the space.** Chairs in a strict circle. No tables. The talking piece visible in the center.

Session Outline (2–2.5 hours):

Segment	Time	Activity
Opening	10 min	Welcome, introductions, review objectives
Key Concepts	20 min	Present and discuss key concepts
Reflection Questions	15 min	Individual writing, paired sharing
Justice Comparison Table	20 min	Small group work on Exercise 1
Identifying Stakeholders	15 min	Large group discussion of Exercise 2
Break	10 min	
Circle Practice	45 min	"When I Was Not Heard"

Segment	Time	Activity
Debrief	10 min	Process the circle experience
Kitchener Case Study	10 min	Discuss case analysis
Assignment & Clos-ing	5 min	Review assignment, closing words

Key Teaching Points to Emphasize:

1. **The paradigm shift is foundational.** Participants must understand that restorative justice is not just a "kinder, gentler" version of retributive justice but a fundamentally different way of thinking about crime and justice.
2. **Harm is relational.** Crime damages relationships—between victim and offender, within communities, and within individuals themselves. Repair must address all these dimensions.
3. **The injustice gap is real and measurable.** The psychological research is not abstract; it describes what participants may have experienced themselves.
4. **Restorative justice is not soft.** It demands more of offenders (active accountability) and communities (active involvement) than conventional justice.

5. **This work requires personal transformation.** Participants cannot facilitate restorative processes for others without doing their own inner work.

Common Questions and Responses:

- **Q: "Isn't this just letting offenders off easy?"**
A: Restorative justice demands more of offenders—confronting victims, understanding impact, making amends—not less. It's often harder than passive punishment.
- **Q: "What about serious crimes like murder?"**
A: Restorative justice has been used successfully even in cases of severe violence, including homicide. It does not replace punishment but can address dimensions punishment cannot reach.
- **Q: "Does this require victims to forgive?"**
A: No. Forgiveness cannot be required or coerced. Restorative justice creates conditions where forgiveness may become possible, but it is never demanded.
- **Q: "I'm not religious. Is this still for me?"**
A: Absolutely. While restorative justice has theological roots, its principles are grounded in universal human needs and validated by empirical research across cultures.

After the Session:

- Send a follow-up email with key takeaways and the assignment
- Check in with any participants who seemed distressed
- Reflect on what worked and what could be improved
- Prepare for Chapter 2: The Principles of Restorative Justice Circles

Key Terms Glossary for Chapter 1

Term	Definition
Retributive Justice	Justice focused on determining guilt and imposing proportionate punishment
Restorative Justice	Justice focused on identifying harm, addressing needs, and repairing relationships
Paradigm Shift	A fundamental change in underlying assumptions and frameworks
Injustice Gap	The discrepancy between a victim's desired resolution and the actual outcome
Stakeholders	All parties affected by harm (victims, offenders, communities)
Shalom	Hebrew concept of comprehensive well-being through right relationship
Imago Dei	Latin for "image of God"; the belief that all humans bear God's image

Term	Definition
Jubilee	Biblical practice of systemic restoration every 50 years
Ubuntu	African philosophy: "A person is a perscn through persons"
VORP	Victim-Offender Reconciliation Program, first established in Kitchener, 1974

"The restorative cycles of creation await our participation. The God of reconciliation calls us to join the divine work of making all things new." — Dr. Maxwell Shimba

CHAPTER 02

The Principles of Restorative Justice Circles

Learning Objectives

By completing this chapter, you will be able to:

- **Identify and explain** the six core principles of restorative justice circles
- **Understand the interdependence** of these principles
- **Recognize** when principles are missing or misapplied
- **Apply** the principles to real-world situations
- **Design** restorative agreements that embody all six principles

---

Core Principles Checklist

☐	Principle	Core Meaning
☐	**Inclusivity**	All affected parties participate in the process
☐	**Voluntariness**	No coercion; free and informed consent required
☐	**Respect and Equality**	Every voice carries equal value; all treated with dignity
☐	**Accountability**	Active responsibility for harm and repair
☐	**Reparation**	Tangible actions to address harm and meet needs
☐	**Reintegration**	Restoration to full community membership

Key Concepts from Chapter 2

Introduction: The Moral Architecture of Restoration

The six principles are not arbitrary procedural preferences. They constitute a **moral architecture**—a coherent framework of ethical commitments that define restorative justice and distinguish it from all other approaches to harm and conflict. These principles are interdependent; each requires and supports the others.

The principles correspond to the fundamental **restorative cycles** woven into biological life:

- Just as the body requires comprehensive engagement of all systems to heal, restorative justice requires **inclusivity**
- Just as healing cannot be coerced but must be endogenously activated, restorative justice requires **voluntariness**
- Just as every cell participates equally in regeneration, restorative justice requires **respect and equality**
- Just as healing requires acknowledgment of injury, restorative justice requires **accountability**
- Just as healing requires active tissue repair, restorative justice requires **reparation**
- Just as healing culminates in restored function, restorative justice requires **reintegration**

PRINCIPLE 1: INCLUSIVITY

Definition: All parties affected by harm have not only a right but a need to participate in the process of resolution.

Theological Foundation: The covenant community of Israel was constituted by divine inclusion. Paul declares, "If one member suffers, all suffer together" (1 Corinthians 12:26). No member can be excluded from the work of restoration.

Legal Framework: International human rights law affirms victims' rights to participate in justice processes. The UN Declaration of Basic Principles of Justice for Victims (1985) encourages "informal mechanisms for the resolution of disputes, including mediation, arbitration and customary justice or indigenous practices."

Philosophical Ground: Inclusivity enables **moral imagination**—the capacity to envision justice as equitable discernment in particular cases. When only the state and offender participate, the range of perspectives is severely limited.

Psychological Dimension: Victims experience profound isolation after harm. Being heard by those who caused the harm and by community is profoundly therapeutic. Research demonstrates that 84.8% of restorative justice participants experience positive psychological changes.

Restorative Cycles: Just as wound healing requires comprehensive engagement of multiple body systems, restorative justice requires participation of all affected parties.

Key Questions for Practice:

- Who has been affected by this harm?
- Who is missing from this process?
- What barriers might prevent their participation?
- How can we ensure their voice is truly heard?

PRINCIPLE 2: VOLUNTARINESS

Definition: No person should be coerced into participation. All participants must choose freely, with adequate information, and may withdraw at any time.

Theological Foundation: The God revealed in Scripture does not coerce relationship but invites it. The father in the prodigal son parable waits, watches, and welcomes—but does not pursue or compel.

Legal Framework: The UN Basic Principles require "free and voluntary consent of the parties" and the right to withdraw at any time. Informed consent requires that participants understand:

- The nature of the process
- Potential outcomes
- Their rights
- The relationship to conventional justice

Philosophical Ground: Coerced accountability is not genuine accountability—it is merely compliance. Apologies offered under pressure are strategic communications, not expressions of remorse.

Psychological Dimension: Cognitive dissonance theory shows that when individuals choose freely, they experience pressure to align beliefs with behavior. Coerced participation produces no such transformation.

Restorative Cycles: Healing cannot be commanded. Sleep, wound healing, and tissue repair follow their own rhythms. Facilitators create conditions for healing but cannot force it.

Key Questions for Practice:

- Is this participant choosing freely, or feeling pressured?
- Do they understand what they are consenting to?
- Have they been informed of their right to withdraw?

- Are there subtle coercive dynamics at work?

PRINCIPLE 3: RESPECT AND EQUALITY

Definition: Every participant possesses intrinsic dignity and deserves equal respect. The circle embodies this through spatial arrangement, the talking piece, and procedural fairness.

Theological Foundation: The *imago Dei*—every human being bears the image of God. This dignity cannot be diminished by sin, damaged by suffering, or forfeited by wrongdoing.

Legal Framework: Equality before the law is a foundational norm. Procedural justice research demonstrates that satisfaction depends more on perceived fairness than on outcome favorability.

Philosophical Ground: Recognition—the affirmation of equal moral worth—is a fundamental human need. Misrecognition (disrespect, degradation, exclusion) is itself a form of harm.

Psychological Dimension: The experience of being treated with respect and having one's voice heard is consistently associated with positive outcomes across contexts. Procedural justice includes:

- Voice – opportunity to participate
- Neutrality – impartial decision-makers
- Respect – treatment with dignity
- Trust – perception of benevolent motives

Restorative Cycles: Every cell in the body contains the complete genome; every cell contributes to the whole. The body is organized through networks of mutual dependence, not chains of command.

Key Questions for Practice:

- Are all participants being treated with equal dignity?
- Does the physical arrangement reflect equality?
- Are some voices dominating while others are silenced?
- How can we ensure the most marginalized voice is heard?

PRINCIPLE 4: ACCOUNTABILITY

Definition: Accountability means active engagement—confronting the human consequences of one's actions, listening to victims, acknowledging responsibility, and undertaking concrete actions to repair harm.

Theological Foundation: Zacchaeus models restorative accountability: "If I have cheated anyone, I will repay it fourfold" (Luke 19:8). This exceeds legal requirements and demonstrates genuine transformation.

Legal Framework: Accountability in restorative justice differs from liability for punishment. It requires active engagement in repairing harm, not passive endurance of sanctions.

Philosophical Ground: Jean Hampton argues that wrongdoing communicates a false message of superiority over the victim. Restorative accountability invites offenders to repudiate this claim voluntarily.

Psychological Dimension: John Braithwaite distinguishes between:

- **Stigmatizing shame** – "I am a bad person" (increases recidivism)

- **Reintegrative shame** – "I did a bad thing" (reduces recidivism)

Restorative circles enact reintegrative shaming—condemning the behavior while respecting the person and offering pathways to repair.

Restorative Cycles: The inflammatory phase of wound healing is the body's acknowledgment of injury. Without inflammation, healing cannot begin. Accountability is the social equivalent—acknowledgment that mobilizes resources for repair.

Key Questions for Practice:

- Is the offender taking genuine responsibility or merely complying?
- Have they heard and understood the victim's experience?
- What concrete actions will demonstrate accountability?
- How can we support rather than stigmatize?

PRINCIPLE 5: REPARATION

Definition: Harm must be repaired through tangible actions that address material, emotional, and relational consequences. Restorative justice requires concrete reparation, not merely symbolic gestures.

Theological Foundation: The Year of Jubilee (Leviticus 25) mandated systemic restoration—debts forgiven, land returned, slaves liberated. Zacchaeus's fourfold restitution exceeds legal requirements.

Legal Framework: The UN Basic Principles define restorative outcomes as agreements aimed at "reparation, restitution and community service." Victims have a right to reparation under international law.

Philosophical Ground: Reparation is moral communication. Restitution communicates recognition of the victim's rights. Apology communicates understanding of harm. Community service communicates willingness to contribute positively.

Psychological Dimension: Receiving reparation reduces the injustice gap, lowers stress, and promotes healing. Making reparation reduces guilt and shame, restores moral agency, and strengthens prosocial commitment.

Restorative Cycles: The proliferative phase of wound healing involves active tissue reconstruction. Reparation is the proliferative phase of social healing—the tangible work of rebuilding what was damaged.

Key Questions for Practice:

- What has been lost or damaged?
- What does the victim need to heal?
- What is the offender capable of providing?
- How can reparation be meaningful and achievable?

PRINCIPLE 6: REINTEGRATION

Definition: Offenders, having taken responsibility and made reparation, are welcomed back into full community membership. This is not return to the status quo ante but creation of new relationships marked by knowledge of both harm and forgiveness.

Theological Foundation: The prodigal son is not merely permitted to return but celebrated with robe, ring, and feast. The community is called to share in the father's joy.

Legal Framework: International law recognizes rehabilitation and social reintegration as goals of justice. "Ban the box" policies and certificates of rehabilitation reflect this commitment.

Philosophical Ground: Reintegration is a gift, not something earned. It is extended in response to demonstrated commitment but remains a gift—something that cannot be demanded but only received with gratitude.

Psychological Dimension: Desistance—ceasing to offend—requires identity transformation and strengthened social bonds. Offenders who experience community welcome are more likely to sustain change.

Restorative Cycles: The remodeling phase of healing strengthens and integrates new tissue. Reintegration is the remodeling phase of social healing—the offender's identity as community member is consolidated and trust is strengthened.

Key Questions for Practice:

- How will the community demonstrate welcome?
- What support does the returning person need?
- What barriers to reintegration exist (employment, housing, stigma)?
- How can the community address these barriers?

The Interdependence of Principles

If you have...	But lack...	The result is...
Inclusivity	Voluntariness	Coercion, not inclusion
Voluntari-ness	Inclusivity	Privilege for the powerful
Respect	Accountabil-ity	Indulgence without responsi-bility
Accountabil-ity	Reparation	Words without action
Reparation	Reintegration	Abandonment after payment
All princi-ples	Faithful prac-tice	Restorative justice

The six principles are not independent requirements. They are interdependent dimensions of a single vision: justice that heals rather than wounds, restores rather than destroys, and reconciles rather than alienates.

Reflection Questions

1. Which principle do you find hardest to practice—and why?

Be honest with yourself. Is it inclusivity when you're angry with someone? Voluntariness when you're sure someone "needs" this process? Respect when the offender seems unrepentant? Accountability when it's easier to blame? Reparation when it costs you? Reintegration when you're still afraid?

2. Think of a conflict you've experienced or witnessed. Which principles were present? Which were missing? What was the result?

3. Inclusivity requires identifying all affected parties. Who might be invisible in a typical justice process? Who is often forgotten?

4. Voluntariness can be compromised by subtle pressure. What might "subtle coercion" look like in a restorative context?

- From justice system officials?
- From family members?
- From facilitators?
- From one's own guilt or fear?

5. Respect and equality are easy to affirm in theory, difficult to practice. When have you seen someone treated with disrespect in the name of "justice"? What was missing?

6. Accountability without reparation is hollow. Describe a situation where someone "took responsibility" verbally but did nothing to make it right. How did that feel?

7. Reparation without reintegration is abandonment. Have you ever seen someone "pay their debt" but remain excluded? What did that communicate?

8. Which principle do you most need to grow in? What would growth in this principle look like in your daily life?

Exercise 1: Principle Mapping (Group Exercise)

Purpose: To deepen understanding of each principle by examining its absence, misuse, and protection.

Time: 45–60 minutes

Format: Small groups (4–6 people per group)

Instructions:

1. Divide participants into six groups (or fewer groups with multiple principles per group).
2. Assign each group one principle: Inclusivity, Voluntariness, Respect/Equality, Accountability, Reparation, or Reintegration.
3. Each group discusses and answers the three questions below for their assigned principle.
4. Groups record their answers on flip chart paper.
5. Each group presents their findings to the large group (5 minutes per group).
6. Large group discussion follows all presentations.

Questions for Each Group:

Question	Prompt
What happens when this principle is missing?	Describe a scenario where this principle is absent. What goes wrong? Who is harmed? What is the outcome?
What does misuse of this principle look like?	Describe a scenario where this principle is invoked but distorted—used to manipulate, exclude, or harm rather than restore.
How can it be protected?	What practices, safeguards, or attitudes protect this principle? How can facilitators ensure it is honored?

Flip Chart Template:

Principle: ______________
When Missing:
When Misused:

Principle: ____________
How Protected:

Discussion Questions for Large Group Debrief:

- Were there common themes across principles?
- Which principle seemed easiest to understand? Hardest?
- Which principle seemed most vulnerable to misuse?
- How do these principles support one another?

Exercise 2: Principle Identification

Purpose: To practice identifying the six principles in action.

Instructions: Read each scenario below. Identify which restorative justice principle(s) are illustrated. Explain your reasoning.

Scenario 1: Before the circle begins, the facilitator meets individually with each participant to explain the process, answer questions, and ensure they understand their right to withdraw at any time.

Principle(s): ________________________________

Why: ____

Scenario 2: The circle includes not only the victim and offender but also their family members, friends, and neighbors who were affected by the incident.

Principle(s): ______________________________

Why: ____

Scenario 3: During the circle, a talking piece is passed so that each person may speak without interruption. The facilitator ensures that quieter participants are invited to share and that no one dominates.

Principle(s): ______________________________

Why: ____

Scenario 4: An offender listens to the victim describe how the crime affected her life. He acknowledges his responsibility and says, "I didn't understand until now how much pain I caused."

Principle(s): ______________________________

Why: ____

Scenario 5: The circle agrees that the offender will pay restitution for damaged property, write a letter of apology, and complete 40 hours of community service.

Principle(s): ______________________________

Why: ____

Scenario 6: Months after completing his obligations, the offender is welcomed back to community events. Neighbors greet him by name and include him in neighborhood activities.

Principle(s): ______________________________

Why: ____

Exercise 3: Principles in Tension

Purpose: To explore how principles can conflict and require discernment.

Instructions: Read each scenario. Discuss how you would navigate the tension between principles.

Scenario A: Voluntariness vs. Accountability

A young offender is reluctant to participate in a restorative circle. He admits what he did but is terrified of facing the victim. His probation officer says if he doesn't participate, he'll be charged and likely incarcerated. The victim wants to meet him.

- How do you honor **voluntariness** when there are real consequences for non-participation?
- How do you honor **accountability** when the alternative is more punitive?
- What would you do?

____

____

____

____

Scenario B: Inclusivity vs. Safety

A victim of domestic violence wants to participate in a restorative circle with her abuser. She believes it will help her heal. The facilitator is concerned about power imbalances and potential re-traumatization. The offender has expressed remorse and willingness to participate.

- How do you honor **inclusivity** (the victim's desire to participate)?
- How do you honor **safety** (protecting from further harm)?

- What would you do?

Scenario C: Reparation vs. Capacity

An offender agrees to pay restitution but has no job and limited income. The victim needs the money to repair damage. A well-meaning community member offers to pay the restitution on the offender's behalf.

- How do you honor **reparation** (the victim's need)?
- How do you honor **accountability** (the offender's responsibility)?
- If someone else pays, has accountability occurred?
- What would you do?

Scenario D: Reintegration vs. Community Readiness

An offender has completed all restorative obligations—restitution, community service, apology. But neighbors remain fearful and angry. They don't want him at community events. They say they're not ready to welcome him back.

- How do you honor **reintegration** (the offender's restoration)?
- How do you honor **community** (their genuine fear and anger)?
- Can reintegration occur without community welcome?
- What would you do?

Circle Practice: "The Principle I Struggle With"

Purpose: To deepen personal engagement with the principles through shared reflection.

Time: 45–60 minutes

Materials: Talking piece, comfortable seating in a circle

Opening (5 minutes):

- Welcome participants.
- Remind of confidentiality.
- Introduce the prompt: "Which of the six principles do I find hardest to practice—and why?"

Check-In Round (10 minutes):

- Pass the talking piece. Each person shares their name and one word about how they're arriving.

Sharing Round (20–30 minutes):

- Pass the talking piece. Each person who wishes responds to the prompt.
- Allow silence between speakers.
- No cross-talk or response.

Reflection Round (10 minutes):

- Pass the talking piece. Each person shares: "What was it like to name my struggle?"

Closing (5 minutes):

- Thank participants.
- Affirm the courage it takes to name struggles.
- Close with a moment of silence.

Case Study Analysis: The Small Town Assessment

Background: (From Chapter 4, but relevant to principles)

A small town experiencing rising youth delinquency and community conflicts conducted a comprehensive community assessment. Local leaders engaged stakeholders, collected diverse data, analyzed findings, developed recommendations, and built support for restorative implementation.

The Process:

- Residents who had felt ignored by local authorities experienced acknowledgment
- Youth who had been labeled "delinquents" were invited to share their perspectives
- Law enforcement officers were engaged as partners
- School officials, law enforcement, youth organizations, and residents sat together in focus groups
- The discovery that the community lacked constructive activities for youth reframed delinquency from individual moral failure to collective responsibility
- Recommendations were developed collaboratively by community stakeholders

Questions:

1. **Inclusivity:** Who was included in this process? Who might still have been missing? How did inclusivity strengthen the outcome?

---

2. **Voluntariness:** Was participation voluntary? What might have motivated different stakeholders to participate?

3. **Respect and Equality:** How did the process demonstrate respect for diverse voices? How were power imbalances addressed?

4. **Accountability:** How did the process shift accountability from individual youth to the whole community? What does "community accountability" mean?

5. **Reparation:** What needed to be repaired in this community beyond the immediate vandalism? What did the recommendations seek to restore?

6. **Reintegration:** How did the process seek to reintegrate youth into the community? How did it seek to reintegrate community trust?

7. **Interdependence:** How did these principles work together in this case? What would have been lost if any principle had been missing?

Practical Assignment: Design a Circle Agreement

Purpose: To apply all six principles by designing a restorative agreement for a specific scenario.

Instructions:

1. Read the scenario below (or use a real situation you have experienced or know about).
2. Design a complete restorative circle agreement that reflects all six principles.
3. Use the template provided.
4. Be specific—include concrete actions, timelines, and responsibilities.
5. After completing the agreement, write a brief reflection explaining how each principle is embodied.

Scenario:

*Maria, a 16-year-old student, was caught vandalizing school property. Over several weeks, she spray-painted graffiti on school walls, causing approximately $2,000 in damage. Maria has been in trouble before for minor infractions but has never been involved in the justice system. The school's zero-tolerance policy calls for expulsion and police involvement.

The school is considering a restorative approach instead. Maria has expressed remorse and willingness to make amends. The custodian who had to clean the graffiti is angry and wants Maria to understand the impact of her actions. Several students witnessed the vandalism and feel the school is less safe. Maria's mother is a single parent working two jobs and is struggling to respond.

Restorative Circle Agreement Template

Date of Circle: ______________

Participants:

Name	Role (victim, offender, supporter, etc.)

Harm Addressed:

Acknowledgment of Responsibility:

(The offender's statement acknowledging what they did and the impact)

Agreed Actions:

Action	Responsible Party	Deadline	Verification

Support Commitments:

(What will community members, family, or others do to support the offender and victim?)

Follow-Up Plan:

(When and how will progress be reviewed?)

Signatures:

_________________________ (Offender)

_________________________ (Victim)

_________________________ (Facilitator)

_________________________ (Community Representative)

Reflection on the Agreement

After completing the agreement, answer these questions:

1. Inclusivity: Who is included in this agreement? Are all affected parties represented? How does the agreement ensure their voices were heard?

2. Voluntariness: How does this agreement reflect voluntary participation? What would indicate coercion?

3. Respect and Equality: How does this agreement demonstrate equal respect for all parties? How are power imbalances addressed?

4. Accountability: What does this agreement require of the offender beyond passive consequences? How does it promote genuine responsibility?

5. Reparation: What tangible actions repair the harm? How do they address material, emotional, and relational dimensions?

6. Reintegration: How does this agreement welcome the offender back into community? What support is provided for ongoing restoration?

7. Interdependence: How do the principles work together in this agreement? What would be missing if any principle were absent?

Facilitator Notes for Chapter 2

Before the Session:

1. **Read Chapter 2 thoroughly.** The principles are the foundation for all restorative practice. Ensure you understand not only each principle but their interdependence.
2. **Prepare for Principle Mapping exercise.** Divide participants into groups in advance. Prepare flip charts with the three questions.
3. **Gather materials:**
    - Talking piece
    - Flip chart paper and markers for each group
    - Copies of the Agreement Template
    - Scenarios printed for Exercises 2 and 3

Session Outline (2.5–3 hours):

Segment	Time	Activity
Opening	10 min	Welcome, check-in, review objectives
Key Concepts	20 min	Present the six principles and their interdependence
Reflection Questions	15 min	Individual writing on "hardest principle"
Principle Mapping	45 min	Small group work on assigned principles
Presentations	30 min	Groups share findings (5 min each)
Break	10 min	
Principles in Tension	25 min	Small group discussion of tension scenarios

Segment	Time	Activity
Circle Practice	30 min	"The Principle I Struggle With"
Agreement Design	30 min	Introduce assignment; begin if time allows
Closing	5 min	Review assignment, closing words

Key Teaching Points:

1. **Principles are interdependent.** They cannot be practiced in isolation. Inclusivity without voluntariness is coercion; accountability without reparation is hollow.
2. **Principles are not abstract ideals.** They must be embodied in concrete practices—the talking piece, preparation meetings, follow-up, etc.
3. **Principles create tension.** Faithful practice requires discernment, not rigid rule-following. The principles guide discernment but do not eliminate the need for wisdom.
4. **Principles protect against misuse.** When something feels wrong in a circle, it's often because a principle is being violated. The principles provide a diagnostic framework.
5. **Principles apply to facilitators too.** Facilitators must model the principles—respecting all participants, being

accountable for their own actions, reintegrating themselves after mistakes.

Common Questions:

- **Q: "What if a victim doesn't want to participate?"** A: Voluntariness applies to victims too. They cannot be compelled. The circle may proceed with surrogate victims or community representatives, or not at all.
- **Q: "What if an offender won't acknowledge responsibility?"** A: Accountability requires acknowledgment. Without it, restorative justice may not be appropriate. The case may need to proceed through conventional channels.
- **Q: "What if the community won't reintegrate someone?"** A: This is a real challenge. Reintegration requires community willingness. The circle may need to address community fears, provide education, and build gradual pathways.
- **Q: "Can these principles be applied in non-criminal contexts?"** A: Absolutely. The principles apply wherever harm occurs—schools, workplaces, families, organizations.

After the Session:

- Collect agreements if this was an in-class assignment.
- Prepare feedback for the next session.
- Remind participants to complete the agreement design if not finished.

Personal Journal: Chapter 2

Date: ______________

The principle I struggle with most is:

Because:

A time when I experienced a principle being honored:

A time when I experienced a principle being violated:

What I'm learning about the interdependence of principles:

How I want to grow:

A question I'm still holding:

Key Terms Glossary for Chapter 2

Term	Definition
Inclusivity	All affected parties participate in the process
Voluntariness	Free and informed consent; right to withdraw

Term	Definition
Respect	Recognition of inherent dignity of all persons
Equality	Equal value of every voice in the circle
Accountability	Active responsibility for harm and repair
Reparation	Tangible actions to address harm
Reintegration	Restoration to full community membership
Moral Architecture	The coherent framework of ethical commitments defining restorative justice
Procedural Justice	Fairness of the process (voice, neutrality, respect, trust)
Reintegrative Shame	Shame focused on behavior, with respect for person and pathways to repair
Stigmatizing Shame	Shame focused on the person as bad, leading to exclusion

Term	Definition
Injustice Gap	Discrepancy between desired and actual resolution

"*Inclusivity without voluntariness is coercion; voluntariness without inclusivity is privilege; respect and equality without accountability is indulgence; accountability without reparation is incomplete; reparation without reintegration is abandonment.*" — Dr. Maxwell Shimba

CHAPTER 03

The History and Evolution of Restorative Justice

Learning Objectives

By completing this chapter, you will be able to:

- **Trace the historical development** of restorative justice from ancient indigenous practices to modern applications
- **Identify key contributions** from indigenous cultures, faith traditions, and legal reformers
- **Understand the displacement** of restorative justice by centralized state justice systems
- **Explain the modern revival** of restorative justice and its key figures and milestones

- **Articulate lessons** that historical and indigenous practices offer for contemporary justice

Key Concepts from Chapter 3

1. The Eternal Cycle of Restoration

The history of restorative justice is not merely a chronicle of a social movement but the story of humanity's recurring encounter with a truth as ancient as creation: that the universe is ordered toward restoration, not destruction. This truth has been:

- **Inscribed in restorative cycles** of the natural world (seasons, regeneration, healing)
- **Embedded in indigenous wisdom** traditions
- **Revealed in Scripture** testifying to God's reconciling work

2. Indigenous Wellsprings of Restorative Wisdom

Indigenous Tradition	Key Concepts	Practices
Māori (New Zealand)	*Whakawhanaungatanga* – building and maintaining relationships; *utu* – restoration of balance	*Hui* (gathering on *marae*) with elders (*kaumatua*) facilitating; all affected parties participate

Indigenous Tradition	Key Concepts	Practices
First Nations (North America)	The circle as sacred space; interconnectedness of all beings; healing rather than punishment	Healing circles; sentencing circles; elder guidance; talking piece; four directions teachings
African Traditions	*Ubuntu* – "a person is a person through persons"; interconnectedness; communal personhood	Community gatherings; elder facilitation; restitution; reconciliation ceremonies

3. Medieval and Early Modern Periods: Community Justice Before the State

System	Key Features	Restorative Elements
English Common Law	Hue and cry; tithings and frankpledge; communal responsibility	Community pursuit of offenders; collective accountability; compensation to victims (*bot*) and community (*wite*)

System	Key Features	Restorative Elements
Continental Europe	*Wergeld* (man-price); compensatory tariffs; integration with ecclesiastical penance	Detailed compensation tariffs; reconciliation through payment; integration of material and spiritual restoration
Ecclesial Tradition	Penance; confession; satisfaction; reconciliation	Public/private confession; acts of penance; restitution as condition of absolution; goal of restoration

4. The Emergence of the Modern Justice System: The Great Forgetting

Between the twelfth and nineteenth centuries, restorative practices were gradually displaced by:

- **Centralization of state power** – Monarchs asserted exclusive jurisdiction, appropriated fines
- **Reception of Roman law** – Crime redefined as offense against state, not injury to victim
- **Reformation** – Weakened ecclesiastical jurisdiction; secularization of church functions
- **Enlightenment rationalization** – Beccaria, Bentham; punishment justified by deterrence, proportionality

Consequences:

- Victims excluded from process
- Offenders became passive recipients of punishment
- Communities reduced to spectators
- Justice became a zero-sum game of suffering

5. The Revival of Restorative Justice: The Return of Ancient Wisdom

Period	Key Developments
1974	Kitchener, Ontario – first Victim-Offender Reconciliation Program (VORP) initiated by Mennonite Central Committee
1989	New Zealand's Children, Young Persons, and Their Families Act – family group conferencing; Māori traditions recognized
1990	Howard Zehr publishes *Changing Lenses* – articulates restorative paradigm shift
1990s-2000s	Expansion throughout world; research demonstrates effectiveness
2002	UN Basic Principles on the Use of Restorative Justice Programmes in Criminal Matters

Period	Key Developments
2012	EU Victims' Rights Directive – requires access to restorative justice services

6. Key Figures in the Restorative Justice Movement

Figure	Contribution
Howard Zehr	"Grandfather of restorative justice"; *Changing Lenses* articulated paradigm shift
Kay Pranis	Foremost practitioner and teacher of restorative justice circles; integrated indigenous wisdom
Mennonite Central Committee	Institutional birthplace of modern restorative justice; VORP programs
Restorative Justice Council (UK)	Professionalization and quality assurance; training standards and accreditation

Figure	Contribution
International Institute for Restorative Practices	Graduate education; restorative practices continuum

7. Expanding Applications

Domain	Applications
Criminal Justice	Victim-offender mediation; family group conferencing; sentencing circles; diversion programs
Education	Restorative schools; alternative to zero-tolerance discipline; community-building circles
Workplace	Conflict resolution; organizational culture; addressing grievances
Community	Neighborhood disputes; public housing; community-based justice

Domain	Applications
Environmental Justice	Addressing pollution, resource conflicts, ecological harm
Healthcare	Medical errors; adverse events; patient-provider conflicts

8. Restorative Cycles in History

The history of restorative justice itself manifests restorative cycles:

- **Loss and recovery** – Ancient wisdom suppressed, then recovered
- **Forgetting and remembering** – Indigenous practices forgotten by colonizers, remembered by descendants
- **Fragmentation and reintegration** – Community justice fragmented by state, reintegrated through restorative programs
- **Death and resurrection** – Restorative justice died with state centralization, resurrected in modern movement

Timeline Activity

Purpose: To create a visual representation of restorative justice history, connecting ancient practices to modern developments.

Instructions:

1. Using the information from this chapter, create a timeline of restorative justice history.
2. Include at least **15 significant events, practices, or publications**.
3. Use different colors or symbols to distinguish between:
    - Indigenous practices (green)
    - Faith-based contributions (blue)
    - Legal/policy developments (red)
    - Key publications/figures (purple)
    - Modern applications (orange)
4. Add brief descriptions for each entry (1-2 sentences).
5. After completing the timeline, answer the reflection questions.

Timeline Template:

(Use the space below to draw your timeline. You may also create this on separate paper or digitally.)

```text
Year    Event/Development
----    -----------------
        Ancient  |
                 |
                 |
                 |
                 |
        Medieval|
                 |
                 |
                 |
                 |
        1800s    |
```

```
    |
    |
    |
1900s   |
    |
    |
    |
2000s   |
    |
    |
Present |
```

Events to Include (select at least 15):

Māori *hui* practices	First Nations healing circles	African Ubuntu traditions
Anglo-Saxon hue and cry	*Wergeld* compensation systems	Early church penance
Medieval penitential manuals	Anabaptist church discipline	Rise of state justice (12th c.)
Roman law reception	Enlightenment rationalization	1974 Kitchener VORP

Howard Zehr – *Changing Lenses*	Mennonite Central Committee	New Zealand FGC Act 1989
Kay Pranis – circle practices	UN Basic Principles 2002	EU Victims' Directive 2012
Restorative schools movement	Workplace restorative justice	Environmental restorative justice
First Nations sentencing circles	South African TRC	IIRP founded (2000)

Reflection on Timeline:

1. What patterns do you notice in the timeline? Are there periods of flourishing and decline?

2. How long did restorative practices exist before the modern court system? What does this suggest about their durability?

3. What role have indigenous peoples played in preserving restorative wisdom?

4. How did faith communities contribute to keeping restorative practices alive?

5. What accelerated the modern revival of restorative justice?

6. Where do you see restorative justice going in the next 50 years?

Reflection Questions

1. Why do you think restorative justice existed before modern courts?

Consider: What did pre-modern communities understand about harm, justice, and relationships that modern systems forgot?

2. What was lost when the state took over the administration of justice?

Who benefited from this shift? Who was harmed?

3. Indigenous restorative traditions survived centuries of colonization and suppression. What does their survival teach us about their value and resilience?

4. The modern restorative justice movement emerged from the Mennonite Central Committee—a faith-based organization. Why might faith communities be natural advocates for restorative justice?

5. New Zealand's 1989 reform explicitly incorporated Māori traditions. What conditions allowed this recognition of indigenous wisdom? What can other countries learn from this example?

6. Howard Zehr described restorative justice as a "paradigm shift." Based on this history, what paradigm was being shifted away from? What was being shifted toward?

7. The chapter describes the modern justice system's emergence as "the great forgetting." What was forgotten? How can we remember?

8. Restorative justice is now being applied in new domains—environmental justice, healthcare, corporate governance. What does this expansion suggest about the principles of restorative justice?

Case Study Analysis: Lessons from Indigenous Justice Systems

Purpose: To examine specific indigenous restorative traditions and identify lessons for modern societies.

Instructions: Choose **two** of the indigenous traditions described below. For each, answer the analysis questions. Then compare them in the final section.

Tradition A: Māori (New Zealand)

Key Concepts:

- *Whakawhanaungatanga* – building and maintaining relationships; making kin
- *Whakapapa* – genealogy connecting all things to primal parents (Earth and Sky)
- *Utu* – restoration of balance; often mistranslated as "revenge" but actually compensation and restoration
- *Hui* – gathering on the *marae* (sacred meeting ground)

Practices:

- All affected parties gather on the *marae*
- Elders (*kaumatua*) facilitate the process
- Extended dialogue continues for hours or days
- Emphasis on hearing all perspectives
- Consensus on actions to restore harmony
- Restitution (*utu*) may include material compensation, ceremonial apology, or gift exchange

Modern Influence:

- Incorporated into New Zealand's youth justice system through 1989 Act
- Family group conferencing adopted worldwide

Analysis Questions for Tradition A:

1. What is the role of **place** (*marae*) in Māori restorative justice? How does sacred space affect the process?

2. What is the significance of **genealogy** (*whakapapa*) for understanding harm and restoration?

3. How does the involvement of **elders** differ from the role of judges in conventional courts?

4. What does the mistranslation of *utu* as "revenge" reveal about cultural misunderstandings of restorative justice?

5. What lessons can modern societies learn from Māori restorative traditions?

Tradition B: First Nations (North America)

Key Concepts:

- The circle as sacred space – microcosm of universe
- Four directions teachings – each associated with wisdom, innocence, introspection, truth
- Healing rather than punishment
- Interconnectedness of all beings
- Elders as wisdom-keepers

Practices:

- Healing circles or sentencing circles
- All participants equal in the circle
- Talking piece ensures all voices heard
- Elders guide but do not impose
- Spiritual elements – prayers, ceremonies, smudging
- Address underlying causes (intergenerational trauma, substance abuse, poverty, cultural disconnection)

- Goal: restore balance and harmony to entire web of relationships

Modern Influence:

- Adapted into peacemaking circles used worldwide
- Kay Pranis integrated indigenous wisdom into restorative practice

Analysis Questions for Tradition B:

1. What is the significance of the **circle** as a spatial arrangement? What does it communicate that rows or hierarchies do not?

2. How does the **holistic** focus (addressing underlying causes) differ from conventional justice's focus on the specific offense?

3. What role do **spiritual elements** play in creating conditions for healing?

4. How does the involvement of **elders** differ from professionalized facilitation?

5. What lessons can modern societies learn from First Nations restorative traditions?

Tradition C: African Ubuntu Traditions

Key Concepts:

- *Ubuntu* – "A person is a person through persons" (*umuntu ngumuntu ngabantu*)
- Personhood as communal achievement, not individual possession

- Interconnectedness; one becomes fully human through participation in community
- Wrongdoing ruptures community and diminishes both offender and community

Practices:

- Community gatherings with all affected parties
- Elders or chiefs facilitate toward consensus
- Emphasis on hearing all perspectives
- Acknowledgment of harm
- Restitution, apology, reconciliation ceremonies
- Goal: reintegration of offender into community

Modern Influence:

- South African Truth and Reconciliation Commission (Archbishop Desmond Tutu)
- Ubuntu philosophy informing restorative justice theory

Analysis Questions for Tradition C:

1. What does *Ubuntu* mean for understanding the nature of the person? How does this differ from Western individualism?

2. If a person is a person through persons, what does wrongdoing do to the **offender's humanity**? What does restoration require?

3. How did Archbishop Tutu apply *Ubuntu* to the Truth and Reconciliation Commission?

4. What might *Ubuntu* offer to societies struggling with mass incarceration and social fragmentation?

5. What lessons can modern societies learn from African restorative traditions?

Comparative Analysis

After analyzing two traditions, answer these comparative questions:

1. What common elements do you see across indigenous restorative traditions?

2. How do these traditions differ from conventional Western justice systems?

Indigenous Tradition	Conventional Western Justice

3. What might indigenous traditions offer that conventional justice cannot?

4. What cautions should modern practitioners observe when learning from indigenous traditions? (Consider appropriation, respect, partnership)

5. If you could incorporate one element from indigenous restorative traditions into your own context, what would it be? Why?

Exercise 1: The Great Forgetting – Then and Now

Purpose: To understand the historical shift from restorative to retributive justice and identify its continuing effects.

Part A: Historical Analysis

Read the section on "The Emergence of the Modern Justice System" (pages 134-137) and answer:

1. What factors contributed to the displacement of restorative practices?

Factor	How it contributed
Centralization of state power	
Reception of Roman law	
Reformation	
Enlightenment rationalization	

2. Who gained from this shift? Who lost?

Gained	Lost

3. The chapter describes this as a "great forgetting." What was forgotten? Why "forgetting" rather than simply "change"?

Part B: Contemporary Parallels

Consider: Are similar dynamics operating today? Are there ways that justice systems continue to "forget" victims, communities, or restorative possibilities?

1. In what ways do contemporary justice systems still exclude victims?

2. In what ways do they fail to address community needs?

3. What is being "forgotten" in current criminal justice debates?

4. What movements or practices are helping us "remember" what was lost?

Exercise 2: Key Figures Matching

Match the figure to their contribution.

Figure	Contribution
1. Howard Zehr	A. Developed peacemaking circle practices from indigenous traditions
2. Kay Pranis	B. Chaired South African Truth and Reconciliation Commission

Figure	Contribution
3. Mennonite Central Committee	C. Wrote *Changing Lenses*, articulated restorative paradigm shift
4. Archbishop Desmond Tutu	D. Founded first Victim-Offender Reconciliation Program in 1974
5. New Zealand Parliament (1989)	E. Established graduate education in restorative practices
6. International Institute for Restorative Practices	F. Enacted family group conferencing into youth justice law

Answers: 1.___ 2.___ 3.___ 4.___ 5.___ 6.___

Exercise 3: Milestones in Restorative Justice

Instructions: For each milestone, explain its significance and lasting impact.

Milestone	What happened?	Why is it significant?
1974 Kitchener Experiment		
1989 New Zealand Act		
1990 *Changing Lenses*		
2002 UN Basic Principles		
2012 EU Victims' Directive		

Circle Practice: "Restorative Justice in My Heritage"

Purpose: To connect personal or cultural history with restorative justice themes.

Time: 45–60 minutes

Materials: Talking piece, comfortable seating

Opening (5 minutes):

- Welcome participants.
- Remind of confidentiality.
- Introduce the prompt: "What traditions for addressing harm, resolving conflict, or restoring relationships exist in my family, culture, or community heritage?"

Check-In Round (10 minutes):

- Pass the talking piece. Each person shares name and one word about how they're arriving.

Sharing Round (20–30 minutes):

- Pass the talking piece. Each person who wishes responds to the prompt.
- Examples: Stories from grandparents, cultural practices, religious traditions, family sayings, community rituals.
- Allow silence between speakers.
- No cross-talk or response.

Reflection Round (10 minutes):

- Pass the talking piece. Each person shares: "What did I learn or remember by hearing these stories?"

Closing (5 minutes):

- Thank participants.
- Note the diversity and richness of traditions represented.
- Close with a moment of silence.

Practical Assignment: Interview an Elder

Purpose: To connect with living history and learn from those who remember different approaches to conflict and justice.

Instructions:

1. Identify an elder in your family, community, or faith tradition—someone from an older generation who may remember different ways of addressing harm.
2. Conduct a 20-30 minute interview. Ask about:
    - How conflicts were handled when they were growing up
    - What they were taught about responding to wrongdoing
    - Stories of disputes being resolved in their family or community
    - Whether they see differences between "then" and "now"
    - What they think has been lost or gained
3. Take notes during or immediately after the interview.
4. Write a 1-2 page reflection addressing:
    - What you learned
    - How it connects to restorative justice principles
    - What surprised you
    - What you will carry forward

Interview Notes:

Reflection:

Case Study: The Kitchener Experiment (1974)

Background:

In 1974, in Kitchener, Ontario, two young men went on a vandalism spree, damaging twenty-two properties. They were ordered by a probation officer and judge to meet with their victims and make restitution. The Mennonite Central Committee facilitated these meetings—the first Victim-Offender Reconciliation Program (VORP).

Analysis Questions:

1. What made this experiment possible? Consider the people, the context, and the timing.

2. Why was the Mennonite Central Committee involved? What theological commitments might have motivated them?

3. How did this experiment differ from conventional justice at the time?

4. Why did this experiment spread so quickly? What needs did it address that conventional justice wasn't meeting?

5. What does this origin story suggest about the relationship between faith communities and restorative justice?

6. If you were to design a "Kitchener experiment" for your community today, what would it look like?

Facilitator Notes for Chapter 3

Before the Session:

1. **Read Chapter 3 thoroughly.** The historical sweeɔ is broad—from ancient indigenous practices to contemporary applications. Identify the key turning points you want to emphasize.
2. **Prepare timeline materials.** Have large paper, markers, and printed lists of events if doing a group timeline. Alternatively, prepare a digital timeline tool.

3. **Gather indigenous resources.** If possible, bring images, videos, or guest speakers familiar with indigenous restorative traditions. Approach with respect and humility.
4. **Be aware of sensitivities.** Some participants may have Indigenous heritage or connections to colonized peoples. Create space for their voices without putting them on the spot to "represent."

Session Outline (2.5–3 hours):

Segment	Time	Activity
Opening	10 min	Welcome, check-in, review objectives
Key Concepts	20 min	Present historical overview – indigenous, medieval, displacement, revival
Timeline Activity	30 min	Individual or small group timeline creation
Timeline Sharing	15 min	Share timelines; note patterns
Reflection Questions	15 min	Small group discussion of "Why restorative justice existed before courts"

Segment	Time	Activity
Break	10 min	
Indigenous Case Stud-ies	30 min	Small groups analyze different traditions; report back
Key Figures Matching	10 min	Quick review activity
Circle Prac-tice	25 min	"Restorative Justice in My Heritage"
Assignment Review	5 min	Explain interview assignment
Closing	5 min	Final reflections, closing words

Key Teaching Points:

1. **Restorative justice is ancient.** It did not begin in 1974. Indigenous peoples preserved restorative wisdom for millennia.

2. **The modern state displaced restorative practices.** This was not inevitable progress but a specific historical development with winners and losers.
3. **Faith communities kept restorative practices alive.** The modern movement emerged from faith commitments, not secular criminology.
4. **Indigenous wisdom is not a "resource" to be extracted.** Modern practitioners must approach indigenous traditions with respect, humility, and commitment to partnership, not appropriation.
5. **The history is not over.** We are living in a period of revival and expansion. The next chapter is being written now.

Common Questions:

- **Q: "Why did restorative justice disappear for so long?"**
  A: It didn't entirely—indigenous communities and some faith communities preserved it. But it was displaced from mainstream institutions by state centralization.
- **Q: "Is restorative justice just 'primitive' justice?"**
  A: No. Indigenous systems are sophisticated, not primitive. And modern restorative justice adapts ancient wisdom to contemporary contexts.
- **Q: "How can I learn more about indigenous restorative practices?"**
- A: Seek out indigenous-led organizations, read works by indigenous authors, attend trainings led by indigenous practitioners. Approach with humility and a willingness to learn.
- **Q: "What about other cultural traditions not covered here?"**

A: This chapter highlights a few examples. There are many others—Japanese *chōtei*, Middle Eastern *sulha*, Asian communal practices. The field is rich and diverse.

After the Session:

- Follow up on interview assignment in next session.
- Collect timeline photos if desired.
- Prepare for Chapter 4 on implementation.

Personal Journal: Chapter 3

Date: ______________

What most surprised me about the history of restorative justice:

An indigenous practice I want to learn more about:

What the "great forgetting" teaches me about justice today:

How my own cultural or family history connects to this chapter:

One thing I will remember from this chapter:

A question I'm still holding:

Key Terms Glossary for Chapter 3

Term	Definition
Whakawhanaungatanga	Māori concept of building and maintaining relationships; making kin
Whakapapa	Māori genealogy connecting all things to primal parents
Utu	Māori concept of restoration of balance; often mistranslated as "revenge"
Hui	Māori gathering on the *marae* (sacred meeting ground)
Marae	Māori sacred meeting ground, center of community life
Kaumatua	Māori elders who guide restorative processes
Ubuntu	African philosophy: "A person is a person through persons"

Term	Definition
Wergeld	Germanic compensatory system ("man-price")
Bot	Anglo-Saxon payment to victim
Wite	Anglo-Saxon payment to community or lord
Hue and cry	Anglo-Saxon communal pursuit of offenders
Tith-ings/frank-pledge	Anglo-Saxon system of collective responsibility
VORP	Victim-Offender Reconciliation Program (first in Kitchener, 1974)
FGC	Family Group Conferencing (originated in New Zealand, 1989)
Paradigm shift	Fundamental change in underlying assumptions (Zehr)

Term	Definition
Reintegrative shaming	Braithwaite's concept – condemning act, respecting person
Stigmatizing shaming	Condemning person, leading to exclusion and increased offending

---

"*The history of restorative justice is a history of memory and recovery.*" — Dr. Maxwell Shimba

CHAPTER 04

Implementing Restorative Justice Circles in Communities

Learning Objectives

By completing this chapter, you will be able to:

- **Assess a community's readiness** for restorative justice implementation
- **Identify and map all stakeholders** affected by harm in a given context
- **Build partnerships** with key community institutions and leaders
- **Develop a comprehensive implementation plan** including setting, purpose, facilitators, and safeguards

- **Anticipate and address challenges** in the implementation process
- **Understand implementation as a restorative process** in itself

Key Concepts from Chapter 4

1. Implementation as Participation in Divine Restoration

The implementation of restorative justice circles is not merely a technical exercise but an act of theological significance—participation in God's work of restoring a broken creation. The implementation process itself mirrors restorative cycles:

- **Community assessment** – Diagnosis as the inauguration of healing
- **Building partnerships** – Covenantal collaboration
- **Training facilitators** – Forming agents of reconciliation
- **Creating guidelines** – Establishing liturgical norms

2. The Four Foundations of Faithful Implementation

Foundation	Purpose	Key Question
Community Assessment	Discern the community's wounds, resources, and readiness	"What is the condition of this community?"
Building Partnerships	Establish covenantal relationships for sustainable practice	"Who must be at the table?"

Foundation	Purpose	Key Question
Training Facilitators	Form skilled, wise, and compassionate practitioners	"Who will guide the process?"
Creating Guidelines	Develop procedural frameworks for consistency and safety	"How will we ensure fidelity?"

3. Community Assessment: Discerning the Body's Condition

Community assessment is the foundational act of restorative implementation—the disciplined practice of listening to a community to understand its wounds, resources, and readiness for healing.

Theological Foundation: God is one who listens. "I have surely seen the affliction of my people... and have heard their cry" (Exodus 3:7). Assessment is a form of divine attentiveness.

Key Dimensions to Assess:

Dimen-sion	Questions
Needs	What harms exist? Who is suffering? What is missing?
Assets	What strengths exist? Who are the healers? What re-sources are available?
Readi-ness	Is the community motivated? Does it have capacity? What barriers exist?
Trust	Is there trust among community members? Trust in in-stitutions?
Trauma	What historical or collective trauma affects the commu-nity?
Culture	What are the community's values, norms, and commu-nication styles?

Methods of Assessment:

- Surveys and questionnaires
- Interviews and focus groups
- Community forums and public meetings

- Existing data analysis (crime stats, school data, health indicators)
- Asset mapping
- SWOT analysis (Strengths, Weaknesses, Opportunities, Threats)

4. Building Partnerships: Covenantal Collaboration

Building partnerships for restorative justice is a theological imperative rooted in the triune God—a community of persons whose eternal life is characterized by mutual indwelling and collaborative action.

The Covenant Model:

Covenant	Key Features
Noahic	Unconditional, everlasting commitment to all creation
Abrahamic	Promise secured by divine oath, not human performance
Mosaic	Terms of relationship; Torah as gift and guide
Davidic	Everlasting dynasty through which God's reign established

Covenant	Key Features
New Covenant	Internalized Torah, forgiveness, restored knowledge of God

Potential Partners:

- Schools and educational institutions
- Faith communities
- Law enforcement and justice system agencies
- Social service providers
- Mental health and healthcare organizations
- Businesses and employers
- Neighborhood associations
- Youth organizations
- Cultural and ethnic community organizations
- Government agencies

Memorandum of Understanding (MOU) Elements:

- Shared vision and values
- Roles and responsibilities
- Governance and decision-making
- Resource commitments
- Confidentiality and data sharing
- Conflict resolution procedures
- Duration and termination provisions

5. Training Facilitators: Forming Agents of Reconciliation

Facilitator training is not merely professional education but spiritual formation—the cultivation of persons who embody the character of Christ and can create conditions for others to encounter reconciling grace.

Essential Facilitator Qualities:

- Empathy
- Impartiality
- Patience
- Integrity
- Open-mindedness
- Resilience

Essential Facilitator Skills:

- Active listening
- Effective communication
- Conflict resolution
- Questioning techniques
- Group facilitation
- Cultural competence
- Ethical decision-making

Training Modules:

1. Orientation – The vocation of facilitation
2. Restorative Justice Principles – Core concepts
3. Facilitation Skills – Active listening, communication, questioning
4. Managing Group Dynamics – Safety, balance, conflict
5. Cultural Competence – Diversity, inclusion, humility
6. Ethical Considerations – Confidentiality, impartiality, boundaries
7. Practical Exercises – Role-playing, simulation

8. Advanced Techniques – Complex cases, trauma-informed practice
9. Ongoing Professional Development – Continuous learning

6. Creating Guidelines: Establishing Liturgical Norms

Guidelines are not constraints on the Spirit's freedom but structures that enable faithful, consistent, and sustainable restorative practice.

Elements of Effective Guidelines:

Element	Purpose
Referral procedures	How cases enter the process
Preparation procedures	How participants are readied
Circle facilitation procedures	How circles are conducted
Agreement documentation	How outcomes are recorded
Follow-up procedures	How implementation is supported

Element	Purpose
Confidentiality guidelines	How information is protected
Record-keeping	How accountability is maintained

Guidelines Development Process:

- Collaborative development with all stakeholders
- Drafting in clear, accessible language
- Review and feedback from community
- Formal approval by relevant authorities
- Training and orientation for all users
- Ongoing monitoring and revision

Community Readiness Assessment

Purpose: To evaluate a community's preparedness for restorative justice implementation across multiple dimensions.

Instructions: Rate your community (or a community you know) on each dimension from 1 (low) to 5 (high). Provide specific evidence or observations for each rating.

Dimension	Rating (1-5)	Evidence/ Observations
Trust in Community – Do community members trust one another? Is there social cohesion?		
Trust in Institutions – Do community members trust schools, police, government, and other institutions?		
Willingness to Dialogue – Are people willing to sit together and talk across difference?		
Awareness of Restorative Justice – Do people know what restorative justice is?		
Leadership Support – Do community leaders (formal and informal) support restorative approaches?		

Dimension	Rating (1-5)	Evidence/ Observations
Existing Conflict Resolution Practices – What practices already exist? Are they restorative?		
Cultural Sensitivity – Is the community culturally diverse? Are there mechanisms for cross-cultural understanding?		
Trauma Awareness – Is there recognition of historical or collective trauma?		
Resource Availability – Are there potential resources (funding, space, volunteers, trainers)?		
Readiness for Change – Is the community open to new approaches?		

Total Score: _____ / 50

Interpretation:

Score	Readiness Level	Recommended Action
45-50	High Readiness	Begin implementation with full stakeholder engagement
35-44	Moderate Readiness	Address specific gaps before full implementation
25-34	Low Readiness	Significant relationship-building and education needed
Below 25	Very Low Readiness	Focus on foundational trust-building before introducing restorative justice

Reflection Questions on Assessment:

1. What are your community's greatest strengths for restorative implementation?

2. What are the most significant gaps or barriers?

3. Based on this assessment, what should be your first steps?

4. Who should be involved in addressing the gaps you identified?

Exercise 1: Stakeholder Mapping

Purpose: To identify all individuals, groups, and institutions affected by harm in a given context and determine how they should be engaged.

Instructions:

1. Choose a specific context (your neighborhood, school, workplace, faith community, or a hypothetical community).

2. Identify all stakeholders who would be affected by harm in that context.
3. Place them on the concentric circles diagram below based on their proximity to the harm.
4. For each stakeholder, note:
    - How they might be affected by harm
    - What they might contribute to restoration
    - How they should be engaged in implementation planning

Concentric Circles Model:

text
[OUTER RING]
(Indirectly affected)
[MIDDLE RING]
(Community institutions, services)
[INNER RING]
(Family, close supporters)
[CENTER]
(Direct victim
and offender)

Stakeholder Mapping Template:

Ring	Stake-holder	How Affected by Harm	Contribution to Restoration	Engagement Strategy
Center	Direct victim			
Center	Direct offender			
Inner Ring				
Inner Ring				
Inner Ring				
Middle Ring				

Ring	Stake-holder	How Affected by Harm	Contribution to Restoration	Engagement Strategy
Middle Ring				
Middle Ring				
Outer Ring				
Outer Ring				

Reflection Questions:

1. Were you surprised by how many stakeholders you identified?

2. Which stakeholders are typically forgotten or excluded in conventional responses to harm?

3. How might the needs of different stakeholders conflict? How might they align?

4. Who from this map should be involved in planning restorative implementation?

5. How will you reach stakeholders who are marginalized or hard to engage?

Exercise 2: Partnership Development

Purpose: To practice identifying, approaching, and building partnerships with key community institutions.

Part A: Identifying Potential Partners

Based on your stakeholder map, list at least five potential partner organizations or groups that should be involved in restorative implementation.

Potential Partner	Why They Matter	What They Could Contribute	Potential Concerns
1.			
2.			
3.			
4.			
5.			

Part B: Crafting the Initial Approach

For one of the partners above, draft an initial outreach message (email, letter, or script for a phone call). Include:

- Introduction and relationship-building
- The case for restorative justice (framed in terms of their values)
- Invitation to dialogue (not a demand to join)
- Specific next step

Draft Outreach Message:

Part C: Anticipating Concerns

For the same partner, list at least three concerns they might raise about restorative justice. Then draft a respectful response.

Concern	Respectful Response
1.	
2.	
3.	

Exercise 3: Facilitator Qualities Self-Assessment

Purpose: To reflect on your own readiness to facilitate restorative circles and identify areas for growth.

Instructions: Rate yourself on each quality from 1 (needs significant development) to 5 (strongly evident). Provide evidence and a growth goal.

Quality	Rating (1-5)	Evidence (when have I demonstrated this?)	Growth Goal
Empathy – Ability to understand and share others' feelings			
Impartiality – Ability to treat all parties fairly			

Quality	Rating (1-5)	Evidence (when have I demonstrated this?)	Growth Goal
Patience – Ability to allow process to unfold			
Integrity – Consistency between words and actions			
Open-mindedness – Receptivity to new perspectives			
Resilience – Ability to sustain engagement through challenges			
Active Listening – Ability to hear beyond words			

Quality	Rating (1-5)	Evidence (when have I demonstrated this?)	Growth Goal
Communication – Clarity and respect in speech			
Conflict Resolution – Ability to navigate tensions			
Cultural Competence – Awareness and adaptability			

Reflection:

1. What are your greatest strengths as a potential facilitator?

---

2. What areas most need development?

3. What specific steps will you take to grow in these areas?

4. Who could support you in this growth?

Exercise 4: Guidelines Development

Purpose: To practice developing restorative circle guidelines for a specific context.

Instructions:

1. Choose a context (school, workplace, faith community, neighborhood).
2. Draft guidelines for restorative circles in that context addressing the elements below.
3. Ensure guidelines are clear, accessible, and culturally appropriate.

Guidelines Template:

Context: ____

Purpose of Circles: ______________________________

Guideline Element	Proposed Guidelines
Referral Procedures – How do cases enter the process? Who can refer? What criteria apply?	
Preparation Procedures – How are participants prepared? Who conducts preparation? What is covered?	
Circle Facilitation – How are circles convened? What are facilitator roles? What ground rules apply?	
Agreement Documentation – How are agreements recorded? What must they include?	
Follow-Up Procedures – What happens after the circle? How is implementation monitored?	

Guideline Element	Proposed Guidelines
Confidentiality – What is confidential? What exceptions exist?	
Record-Keeping – What records are kept? Who has access?	

Reflection:

1. How did you ensure these guidelines are culturally appropriate for your chosen context?

2. How would you involve community members in reviewing and approving these guidelines?

3. What challenges might arise in implementing these guidelines consistently?

Practical Assignment: Draft a Community Implementation Plan

Purpose: To synthesize learning from this chapter by developing a comprehensive implementation plan for a real or hypothetical community.

Instructions:

Using the template below, draft a complete implementation plan for restorative justice circles in a specific setting. Be as concrete and detailed as possible.

Community Implementation Plan Template

1. Setting

Element	Description
Community Name/Location	
Community Type (neighborhood, school, workplace, faith community, etc.)	
Population/Size	
Key Characteristics (demographics, culture, history, assets, challenges)	

Element	Description
Existing Conflicts or Harms (what issues make restorative justice needed?)	

2. Purpose and Vision

Element	Description
Vision Statement (What will success look like in 3-5 years?)	
Mission Statement (What will this initiative do?)	
Core Values (What principles will guide implementation?)	
Specific Goals (Measurable objectives for first year)	
- Goal 1	

Element	Description
- Goal 2	
- Goal 3	

3. Community Assessment Summary

Element	Findings
Key Needs Identified	
Key Assets Identified	
Readiness Level (from assessment)	
Primary Gaps to Address	
Cultural Considerations	

4. Stakeholder Engagement

Element	Description
Key Stakeholders (list from mapping exercise)	
Engagement Strategies (how will each be involved?)	
Partnerships to Develop (priority partners)	
Communication Plan (how will information be shared?)	

5. Facilitator Training Plan

Element	Description
Number of Facilitators Needed (first year, long-term)	
Recruitment Strategy (who, how, from where?)	

Element	Description
Initial Training Curriculum (topics, duration, format)	
Trainers (who will provide training?)	
Ongoing Professional Development (supervision, peer learning, advanced training)	
Facilitator Support (self-care, burnout prevention)	

6. Guidelines and Procedures

Element	Description
Referral Procedures	
Preparation Procedures	
Circle Facilitation Procedures	

Element	Description
Agreement Documentation	
Follow-Up Procedures	
Confidentiality Guidelines	
Record-Keeping	

7. Safeguards and Risk Management

Element	Description
Participant Safety (physical, emotional, psychological)	
Voluntariness Protections (how ensured?)	
Confidentiality Protections	
Power Imbalance Safeguards	

Element	Description
Trauma-Informed Practices	
Emergency Procedures (if crisis occurs)	
Liability and Insurance	
Complaint/Grievance Process	

8. Resource Plan

Element	Description
Budget (major categories and amounts)	
Funding Sources (grants, budget allocations, donations, fees)	
In-Kind Resources (volunteers, space, materials)	
Facilities (where will circles be held?)	

Element	Description
Materials Needed	

9. Timeline

Phase	Activities	Timeline	Responsible Parties
Phase 1: Planning			
Phase 2: Building Support			
Phase 3: Training			
Phase 4: Pilot Implementation			
Phase 5: Evaluation & Refinement			

Phase	Activities	Timeline	Responsible Parties
Phase 6: Full Implementation			

10. Evaluation Plan

Element	Description
Outcomes to Measure	
Data Collection Methods	
Evaluation Frequency	
Feedback Mechanisms (participant, facilitator, community)	
Use of Findings (how will data inform improvement?)	

11. Sustainability Plan

Element	Description
Leadership Succession (how will new leaders be developed?)	
Ongoing Training (how will capacity be maintained?)	
Funding Sustainability (beyond initial grants)	
Community Ownership (how will community take ownership?)	

Integration with Existing Systems

Reflection Questions on Implementation

1. What part of this implementation plan feels most challenging? Why?

2. What part feels most exciting? Why?

3. Who in your community would need to be invclved for this plan to succeed?

4. What is the first step you could take toward implementation, even if small?

5. What fears or hesitations do you have about implementing restorative justice?

Circle Practice: "What Our Community Needs"

Purpose: To practice community dialogue about restorative needs and to model the kind of gathering that implementation requires.

Time: 45–60 minutes

Materials: Talking piece, comfortable seating

Opening (5 minutes):

- Welcome participants.
- Remind of confidentiality.
- Introduce the prompt: "What does our community (or a community you care about) need to heal and become more restorative?"

Check-In Round (10 minutes):

- Pass the talking piece. Each person shares name and one word about how they're arriving.

Sharing Round (20–30 minutes):

- Pass the talking piece. Each person who wishes responds to the prompt.
- Encourage specificity: What concrete needs, assets, challenges exist?
- Allow silence between speakers.
- No cross-talk or response.

Reflection Round (10 minutes):

- Pass the talking piece. Each person shares: "What did I learn or notice during this circle?"

Closing (5 minutes):

- Thank participants.
- Note themes that emerged.
- Close with a moment of silence.

Case Study: Small Town Community Assessment

Background:

A small town experiencing rising youth delinquency and community conflicts conducted a comprehensive community assessment. Local leaders engaged stakeholders, collected diverse data, analyzed findings, developed recommendations, and built support for restorative implementation.

The Process:

- Residents who had felt ignored by local authorities experienced acknowledgment
- Youth who had been labeled "delinquents" were invited to share their perspectives
- Law enforcement officers were engaged as partners
- School officials, law enforcement, youth organizations, and residents sat together in focus groups
- The discovery that the community lacked constructive activities for youth reframed delinquency from individual moral failure to collective responsibility
- Recommendations were developed collaboratively by community stakeholders

Analysis Questions:

1. What made this assessment process restorative in itself, not just preparatory?

2. How did the process embody the principle of inclusivity?

3. What was the significance of reframing delinquency from "individual moral failure" to "collective responsibility"?

4. How did engaging diverse stakeholders (including youth and law enforcement) strengthen the process?

5. What lessons from this case study apply to your own context?

Facilitator Notes for Chapter 4

Before the Session:

1. **Read Chapter 4 thoroughly.** The implementation process has many moving parts. Identify which sections are most relevant to your participants' contexts.
2. **Prepare assessment tools.** Have copies of the Community Readiness Assessment and Stakeholder Mapping templates ready.
3. **Gather local knowledge.** If possible, research your own community's assets, challenges, and potential partners to share examples.
4. **Identify potential guest speakers.** If you know someone who has implemented restorative justice in a community, consider inviting them to share.

Session Outline (3–3.5 hours):

Segment	Time	Activity
Opening	10 min	Welcome, check-in, review objectives
Key Concepts	25 min	Present four foundations of implementation
Community Readiness Assessment	20 min	Individual assessment, small group discussion
Stakeholder Mapping	25 min	Individual or small group mapping
Break	10 min	
Partnership Development	20 min	Exercise on identifying and approaching partners
Facilitator Qualities	15 min	Self-assessment and reflection

Segment	Time	Activity
Guidelines Development	20 min	Small group work on guidelines
Implementation Plan	30 min	Introduce template; begin drafting if time
Circle Practice	20 min	"What Our Community Needs"
Closing & Assignment	10 min	Review implementation plan assignment

Key Teaching Points:

1. **Implementation is itself restorative.** The process of assessing, partnering, training, and creating guidelines should embody restorative principles.
2. **Start where the community is.** Assessment reveals readiness; don't force implementation where foundations aren't laid.
3. **Partnerships are covenantal, not contractual.** They require ongoing commitment, not just signed agreements.
4. **Facilitators are formed, not just trained.** Qualities matter as much as skills; formation requires time and support.

5. **Guidelines enable, not restrict.** Clear procedures create safety and consistency that free participants to engage vulnerably.

Common Questions:

- **Q: "What if our community isn't ready?"**
  A: Readiness assessment tells you where to start. Low readiness means focus on relationship-building and education before implementation.
- **Q: "How do we find facilitators?"**
  A: Recruit from diverse community sectors—faith communities, schools, social services, volunteers. Look for people with natural restorative qualities.
- **Q: "What if partners disagree?"**
  A: Disagreement is normal. Build conflict resolution into partnership agreements. Use restorative principles to address partnership conflicts.
- **Q: "How long does implementation take?"**
  A: There's no single timeline. Thorough assessment and relationship-building may take months or years. Rushing leads to failure.
- **Q: "What if we have no funding?"**
  A: Start with volunteer facilitators, donated space, and in-kind resources. Demonstrate value before seeking grants.

After the Session:

- Collect implementation plans for feedback.
- Connect participants with local restorative justice initiatives if available.
- Prepare for Chapter 5 on facilitator roles.

Personal Journal: Chapter 4

Date: _______________

The most important thing I learned about implementation:

A community I care about and its readiness for restorative justice:

A potential partner I want to reach out to:

My own readiness to facilitate (strengths and growth areas):

One step I will take toward implementation:

A question I'm still holding:

Key Terms Glossary for Chapter 4

Term	Definition
Community Assessment	The process of discerning a community's needs, assets, and readiness for restorative justice

Term	Definition
Asset Mapping	Identifying community strengths and resources, not just deficits
SWOT Analysis	Assessment of Strengths, Weaknesses, Opportunities, and Threats
Stakeholder	Any person or group affected by harm or with a stake in its resolution
Stakeholder Mapping	Identifying and analyzing all parties affected by harm
Memorandum of Understanding (MOU)	Formal agreement between partner organizations
Subsidiarity	Principle that decisions should be made at the most local level possible
Solidarity	Commitment to the common good and to the well-being of all

Term	Definition
Phronesis	Practical wisdom; capacity to discern what justice requires in particular situations
Paideia	Comprehensive formation of the whole person (Greek concept)
Covenant	Solemn commitment to faithful relationship, distinguished from contract
Incarnational Presence	Being physically present in community, not just conducting business from a distance
Provisional Matrix	Temporary structure that scaffolds healing (biological metaphor)

"The implementation of restorative justice circles in communities is a sacred trust. It is the work of translating the vision of restorative justice—a vision rooted in the character of God, the dignity of human persons, and the restorative cycles woven into the fabric of creation—into the concrete practices, structures, and relationships of particular communities." — Dr. Maxwell Shimba

CHAPTER 05

The Role of Facilitators in Restorative Justice Circles

Learning Objectives

By completing this chapter, you will be able to:

- **Identify the essential qualities** of an effective restorative justice facilitator
- **Assess your own readiness** for facilitation across multiple dimensions
- **Develop the core skills** needed for guiding restorative circles

- **Understand the responsibilities** of facilitators before, during, and after circles
- **Practice responding** to challenging participant behaviors and dynamics
- **Recognize the spiritual and vocational dimensions** of facilitation

Key Concepts from Chapter 5

1. The Facilitator as Icon of Divine Presence

The facilitator's role is not merely a function or a set of competencies to be mastered. It is a vocation—a divine calling to participate in the reconciling work of God. The facilitator stands at the threshold of the circle, welcoming the wounded and the wounding, becoming an icon of divine presence—a visible sign of the invisible God who hears the cry of the afflicted and labors for reconciliation.

2. Essential Qualities of Effective Facilitators

Quality	Description	Theological Ground
Empathy	Ability to understand and share others' feelings without being consumed	Participation in divine compassion

Quality	Description	Theological Ground
Impartiality	Treating all participants with equal respect regardless of role or status	Participation in divine justice
Patience	Allowing the process to unfold without rushing toward resolution	Participation in divine forbearance
Integrity	Consistency between words and actions; trustworthiness	Participation in divine faithfulness
Open-mindedness	Receptivity to perspectives that challenge one's assumptions	Participation in divine wisdom
Resilience	Capacity to sustain engagement without being destroyed by suffering	Participation in divine hope

3. Essential Skills of Effective Facilitators

Skill	Description
Active Listening	Hearing not just words but emotions, meaning, and what is left unsaid
Effective Communication	Speaking clearly, respectfully, and in ways that build understanding
Conflict Resolution	Navigating tensions and disagreements constructively
Questioning Techniques	Asking open-ended questions that invite reflection and discovery
Group Facilitation	Managing dynamics, ensuring equal participation, maintaining safety
Cultural Competence	Understanding and respecting diverse cultural backgrounds
Ethical Decision-Making	Navigating dilemmas with wisdom and integrity

4. Responsibilities of Facilitators

Phase	Responsibilities
Preparation	Individual meetings with participants; explaining process; addressing concerns; assessing readiness; building trust
During the Circle	Setting tone; guiding process; maintaining safety; facilitating dialogue; ensuring equal voice; managing emotions
Post-Circle	Documenting agreements; providing support; conducting follow-up; debriefing with co-facilitators

5. The Theological Grounding of Facilitator Responsibilities

Responsibility	Corresponds to	Biblical Model
Preparation	Prophetic office	John the Baptist preparing the way
Guiding the process	Kingly office	Servant leadership of Jesus

Responsibility	Corresponds to	Biblical Model
Facilitating dialogue	Priestly office	Mediating between God and humanity
Post-circle follow-up	Pastoral office	The Good Shepherd caring for sheep

6. The Psychology of Facilitation

- **Empathy** must be balanced with **emotional regulation** – the capacity to manage one's own emotional responses
- **Impartiality** requires awareness of **cognitive biases** (confirmation bias, in-group bias, attribution bias)
- **Patience** requires **tolerance of uncertainty** and capacity for delayed gratification
- **Resilience** requires **realistic expectations**, **social support**, **self-care practices**, and **sense of meaning**

7. The Philosophy of Facilitation: Virtue Ethics

- **Virtues** are cultivated through practice, not just taught
- **The unity of the virtues** – one cannot genuinely possess one virtue without others
- **Phronesis (practical wisdom)** – the capacity to discern what virtue requires in particular situations

- **Techne (skill)** must be integrated with **phronesis** – technique without wisdom is rigid; wisdom without technique is ineffective

8. Restorative Cycles and Facilitation

Biological Process	Facilitator Parallel
Immune cells recognize damage	Empathy recognizes participants' needs
Platelets act impartially	Impartiality toward all participants
Growth factors act with patience	Patience allowing process to unfold
Extracellular matrix provides structure	Integrity provides reliable container
Stem cells differentiate as needed	Open-mindedness adapts to situations
Tissue regenerates with resilience	Resilience sustains through challenges

Self-Assessment: Facilitator Qualities

Purpose: To honestly evaluate your current capacities across the essential facilitator qualities and identify areas for growth.

Instructions: Rate yourself on each quality from 1 (needs significant development) to 5 (strongly evident). For each, provide specific evidence and identify a growth goal.

Quality	Rating (1-5)	Evidence (when have I demonstrated this? When have I struggled?)	Growth Goal
Listening without judgment – Can I hear difficult things without reacting, correcting, or condemning?			
Emotional regulation – Can I stay calm when others are flooded with emotion?			

Quality	Rating (1-5)	Evidence (when have I demonstrated this? When have I struggled?)	Growth Goal
Cultural humility – Do I recognize the limits of my own cultural perspective and remain open to learning?			
Spiritual maturity – Do I have resources (faith, practice, community) that sustain me through difficult work?			
Empathy – Can I feel with others without being consumed?			

Quality	Rating (1-5)	Evidence (when have I demonstrated this? When have I struggled?)	Growth Goal
Impartiality – Can I treat all parties fairly regardless of my feelings about them?			
Patience – Can I allow processes to unfold without rushing?			
Integrity – Are my words and actions consistent?			
Open-mindedness – Am I receptive to perspectives that challenge me?			

Quality	Rating (1-5)	Evidence (when have I demon-strated this? When have I struggled?)	Growth Goal
Resilience – Can I sustain engagement through challenges?			

Reflection:

1. What are your three greatest strengths as a potential facilitator?

2. What are your three most significant growth areas?

3. Which quality will you focus on developing first? Why?

4. Who could support you in this growth (mentor, peer, supervisor)?

Reflection Questions

1. What personal wounds might affect your neutrality as a facilitator?

We all carry wounds. The question is not whether we have them but whether we are aware of them and have done enough healing that they do not unconsciously shape our facilitation. Consider:

- What experiences of victimization might make it hard for you to be impartial with offenders?
- What experiences of causing harm might make it hard for you to be impartial with victims?
- What relationships or identities might trigger strong reactions?
- What fears might affect your ability to stay present?

Write honestly:

2. How will you ensure your wounds do not compromise your facilitation?

3. The chapter describes the facilitator as an "icon of divine presence." What does this mean to you? How does it affect how you understand the role?

4. Which of the seven skills do you find most natural? Which most challenging?

Skill	Natural or challenging?	Why?
Active Listening		
Effective Communication		
Conflict Resolution		
Questioning Techniques		
Group Facilitation		
Cultural Competence		
Ethical Decision-Making		

5. The chapter distinguishes between *techne* (skill) and *phronesis* (practical wisdom). Why is this distinction important for facilitation?

6. What practices sustain you? How will you maintain your own well-being while doing this demanding work?

Exercise 1: Role-Play Practice

Purpose: To practice facilitation skills in response to challenging participant behaviors.

Time: 45–60 minutes

Format: Small groups of 4-6 people. One person serves as facilitator. Others play roles. After each scenario, debrief as a group.

Scenario A: The Defensive Offender

Setting: A restorative justice circle addressing a theft. The offender, Marcus, has acknowledged taking the property but is now becoming defensive.

Role: Marcus (Defensive Offender)

You admitted to the theft but now feel attacked. You keep explaining why you did it—you were desperate, you had no choice, the victim "has plenty." You interrupt when the victim speaks. You say things like:

- "You don't understand my situation."
- "I said I was sorry. What more do you want?"
- "It's not like I hurt anyone."
- "You're all just ganging up on me."

Role: Facilitator

Your task is to:

- Acknowledge Marcus's feelings without endorsing his defensiveness
- Redirect to the impact on the victim
- Maintain ground rules about listening and not interrupting
- Keep the circle safe for the victim
- Help Marcus move toward genuine accountability

Other Participants: Victim, community members (play these roles naturally, reacting to the dynamic)

Debrief Questions:

- How did the facilitator handle the defensiveness?
- What worked? What could have been done differently?
- How did the victim feel during this exchange?
- How did Marcus feel? Did the facilitator's approach help him lower his defenses?

Scenario B: The Angry Victim

Setting: A restorative justice circle addressing a physical assault. The victim, Elena, is facing the person who attacked her.

Role: Elena (Angry Victim)

You are furious. This attack has affected every part of your life—you can't sleep, you're afraid to go out, you've lost trust in people. When the offender speaks, you feel rage. You say things like:

- "You ruined my life and you expect me to just sit here and listen to you?"
- "I don't care about your reasons. There's no excuse."
- "You should be in prison, not in some circle."
- "I want you to feel what I felt."

Role: Facilitator

Your task is to:

- Validate Elena's anger without letting it become destructive
- Help her express her feelings in ways that can be heard

- Protect the offender from verbal attack while holding them accountable
- Keep the circle safe for both parties
- Help Elena move from raw anger to articulation of needs

Other Participants: Offender, community members

Debrief Questions:

- How did the facilitator validate anger without letting it become destructive?
- What was challenging about this scenario?
- How did the offender experience the facilitator's interventions?
- What might Elena need beyond this circle to continue healing?

Scenario C: The Silent Participant

Setting: A restorative justice circle addressing workplace conflict. One participant, James, has said almost nothing for an hour.

Role: James (Silent Participant)

You are overwhelmed. You've never been in a setting like this. You're not sure you can trust these people. You're afraid that if you speak, you'll cry or say something wrong. Every time you think about speaking, your heart races and your mind goes blank.

Role: Facilitator

Your task is to:

- Notice James's silence without putting him on the spot
- Create conditions that might make it easier for him to speak
- Offer invitations, not demands
- Respect his right to remain silent while ensuring he knows his voice matters
- Check in privately if appropriate

Other Participants: Other circle participants (some may be dominating, some may also be quiet)

Debrief Questions:

- How did the facilitator notice and respond to silence?
- What invitations worked? What felt pressuring?
- How did James experience the facilitator's approach?
- What might help in preparation for future circles?

Exercise 2: Active Listening Practice

Purpose: To practice the core skill of active listening.

Time: 20 minutes

Format: Pairs

Instructions:

1. **Partner A speaks for 3 minutes** on a topic of their choice (something meaningful but not too vulnerable—a passion, a challenge at work, a recent experience).
2. **Partner B listens actively:**
    - Maintain eye contact

    - Use nonverbal cues (nodding, leaning in)
    - Do not interrupt
    - Do not plan your response while they speak
    - Notice your internal reactions without acting on them
3. **After 3 minutes, Partner B reflects back** what they heard:
    - Summarize the content
    - Reflect the emotions they observed
    - Ask clarifying questions if needed
    - Do not evaluate, advise, or share your own experience
4. **Partner A gives feedback:**
    - What did Partner B hear accurately?
    - What did they miss?
    - How did it feel to be listened to in this way?
5. **Switch roles and repeat.**

Debrief Questions for Whole Group:

- What was challenging about listening without planning your response?
- What was challenging about reflecting back without evaluating?
- How did it feel to be truly listened to?
- How can you bring this skill into facilitation?

Exercise 3: Questioning Techniques

Purpose: To practice asking open-ended questions that invite reflection and discovery.

Time: 20 minutes

Format: Pairs or small groups

Instructions:

For each scenario below, generate:

- **3 open-ended questions** (cannot be answered with yes/no; invite reflection)
- **1 question to avoid** (closed, leading, or judgmental)

Scenario 1: A victim who has just described the impact of a crime

Open-Ended Questions	Question to Avoid
1.	
2.	
3.	

Scenario 2: An offender who has just acknowledged responsibility

Open-Ended Questions	Question to Avoid
1.	
2.	
3.	

Scenario 3: A community member who is observing the circle

Open-Ended Questions	Question to Avoid
1.	
2.	
3.	

Scenario 4: A participant who is struggling to articulate their feelings

Open-Ended Questions	Question to Avoid
1.	
2.	
3.	

Debrief:

- What makes a question "open-ended"?
- What questions seemed most effective? Why?
- How can you tell if a question is helpful or intrusive?

Exercise 4: Managing Group Dynamics

Purpose: To practice interventions for common group dynamics challenges.

Instructions: For each scenario, write what you would say or do as facilitator.

Scenario 1: Someone keeps interrupting.

What do you say/do?

Scenario 2: One person is dominating, speaking far longer than others.

What do you say/do?

Scenario 3: Two participants are arguing with each other, not using the talking piece.

What do you say/do?

Scenario 4: Someone becomes overwhelmed with emotion and is crying uncontrollably.

What do you say/do?

Scenario 5: A participant makes a blaming, attacking statement.

What do you say/do?

Scenario 6: The circle has gone silent and no one seems to know what to say.

What do you say/do?

Debrief in Small Group:
Share your responses. Discuss:

- What interventions felt natural? Which felt difficult?
- What principles guide your interventions?
- How do you balance maintaining structure with allowing organic dialogue?

Circle Practice: "A Time I Was Not Heard"

Purpose: To practice facilitation in a real circle experience and to experience the vulnerability of sharing.

Time: 45–60 minutes

Materials: Talking piece, comfortable seating

Facilitator Instructions:

Before the circle, choose one participant to serve as facilitator for this practice. (If this is a training group, rotate facilitation roles across sessions.)

Opening (5 minutes):

- Welcome participants.
- Remind of confidentiality.
- Introduce the prompt: "Share a time when you were not heard—when your voice, your experience, or your pain was dismissed, ignored, or invalidated."

Check-In Round (10 minutes):

- Pass the talking piece. Each person shares their name and one word about how they're arriving.

Sharing Round (20–30 minutes):

- Pass the talking piece. Each person who wishes responds to the prompt.
- Allow silence between speakers.
- No cross-talk or response.

Reflection Round (10 minutes):

- Pass the talking piece. Each person shares: "What was it like to share or to listen?"

Closing (5 minutes):

- Thank participants.
- Affirm the courage it took to share.
- Close with a moment of silence.

After the Circle: Debrief the Facilitation

If this was a practice facilitation, debrief with the facilitator afterward:

- What felt natural?
- What was challenging?
- How did you decide when to speak and when to stay silent?
- What would you do differently next time?

Practical Assignment: Facilitator Journal

Purpose: To develop the habit of reflective practice essential for facilitator growth.

Instructions: After each facilitation you observe or conduct (including practice sessions), complete this journal entry.

Date of Circle: ______________

Context: ____

Your Role (observer, co-facilitator, lead facilitator): ______________________________

What happened? (Brief summary)

What went well? (What were you pleased with?)

What was challenging? (What was difficult or uncomfortable?)

What did you learn about yourself as a facilitator?

What did you learn about the participants or the process?

What would you do differently next time?

One question you're holding:

Case Study: The Facilitator's Wounds

Background:

A facilitator named Sarah has been leading restorative circles for three years. She is skilled, experienced, and respected. Five years ago, Sarah's home was burglarized. The offender was never caught. Sarah thought she had processed this experience, but recently she facilitated a circle involving a burglary. During the victim's testimony, Sarah felt her heart racing, her palms sweating, and a surge of anger toward the offender that she struggled to hide. After the circle, she realized she had not been fully present—she had been reacting to her own unresolved experience.

Questions:

1. What happened to Sarah? Why did she react this way?

2. Was Sarah wrong to facilitate this circle? Why or why not?

3. What should Sarah have done differently in preparation?

4. What should Sarah do now?

5. What does this case teach about the relationship between facilitators' wounds and their work?

6. What safeguards might prevent this situation or support a facilitator when it occurs?

Practical Exercise: Developing Your Facilitator Formation Plan

Purpose: To create a personal plan for ongoing growth as a restorative facilitator.

Instructions: Complete each section with specific commitments.

Area	Current State	Growth Goal	Action Steps	Timeline	Support/Resources
Skills (active listening, questioning, etc.)					
Qualities (patience, empathy, etc.)					
Self-Awareness (wounds, triggers, biases)					
Cultural Competence					

Area	Current State	Growth Goal	Action Steps	Timeline	Support/Resources
Self-Care (preventing burnout)					
Supervision/Peer Support					
Spiritual Formation (if applicable)					
Ongoing Education					

Accountability: Who will support you in this plan? How will you check progress?

Facilitator Code of Ethics

Purpose: To articulate the ethical commitments of restorative facilitators.

Instructions: Review the following commitments. Add any that are missing for your context. Then sign as a personal commitment.

As a restorative justice facilitator, I commit to:

☐ **Respect** – Treating all participants with dignity, regardless of their role in the harm

☐ **Impartiality** – Not favoring any party; maintaining fairness throughout the process

☐ **Confidentiality** – Protecting what is shared in circle, with clear exceptions for safety

☐ **Competence** – Continuing to develop my skills and knowledge

☐ **Preparation** – Thoroughly preparing all participants before circles

☐ **Safety** – Prioritizing physical and emotional safety for all

☐ **Voluntariness** – Ensuring participation is free and informed; honoring the right to withdraw

☐ **Empowerment** – Supporting participants' agency, not imposing solutions

☐ **Humility** – Recognizing the limits of my knowledge; remaining open to learning

☐ **Self-Care** – Attending to my own well-being to sustain this work

☐ **Accountability** – Being answerable to participants, programs, and community

☐ **Cultural Humility** – Approaching cultural difference with openness and respect

Additional commitments for my context:

☐ ____

☐ ____

I commit to upholding these principles to the best of my ability.

Signature: ______________________ **Date:** ___________

Facilitator Notes for Chapter 5

Before the Session:

1. **Read Chapter 5 thoroughly.** The facilitator's role is the most personal chapter—participants may have strong reactions.

2. **Prepare for vulnerability.** The self-assessment and reflection questions invite honesty about limitations and wounds. Create a safe container.
3. **Recruit role-play participants in advance.** For the role-play exercise, you may want to brief volunteers on their roles ahead of time.
4. **Gather materials:**
    - Talking piece
    - Copies of self-assessment and role-play scenarios
    - Facilitator Code of Ethics for each participant

Session Outline (3–3.5 hours):

Segment	Time	Activity
Opening	10 min	Welcome, check-in, review objectives
Key Concepts	20 min	Present qualities, skills, responsibilities
Self-Assessment	15 min	Individual completion of facilitator qualities assessment
Reflection Questions	15 min	Small group discussion of personal wounds and neutrality

Segment	Time	Activity
Active Listening Practice	20 min	Pairs exercise
Break	10 min	
Role-Play Scenarios	45 min	Small groups rotate through three scenarios
Debrief Role-Plays	15 min	Large group share insights
Questioning Techniques	15 min	Pairs exercise
Circle Practice	25 min	"A Time I Was Not Heard"
Facilitator Code of Ethics	10 min	Review and sign

Segment	Time	Activity
Closing & Assignment	5 min	Review Facilitator Journal assignment

Key Teaching Points:

1. **Facilitators are not neutral technicians.** They bring their whole selves—including wounds, biases, and gifts. Self-awareness is essential.
2. **Qualities matter as much as skills.** You can teach skills; qualities must be cultivated through practice and formation.
3. **The facilitator's role is limited.** You are responsible for the process, not the outcomes. You cannot force healing, accountability, or forgiveness.
4. **Self-care is not selfish.** It is essential for sustainability. Burned-out facilitators help no one.
5. **Supervision and peer support are essential.** No one should facilitate alone or without ongoing support.

Common Questions:

- **Q: "What if I'm not spiritually mature? Can I still facilitate?"**
  A: "Spiritual maturity" here refers to having resources (whatever your tradition) that sustain you. Everyone needs sources of meaning and renewal.
- **Q: "How do I know if I'm ready to facilitate?"**
  A: Readiness is a process, not a destination. Start with

co-facilitation with an experienced mentor. Get feedback. Continue learning.

- **Q: "What if I make a mistake?"**
  A: You will. Acknowledge it, learn from it, repair any harm caused. Your own accountability models restorative values.
- **Q: "Can I facilitate if I have unresolved trauma?"**
  A: Possibly, with adequate self-awareness, support, and safeguards. Know your triggers. Have a plan. Don't facilitate cases that are too close to your own wounds.
- **Q: "How do I handle participants who trigger me?"**
  A: Preparation helps you anticipate triggers. Grounding techniques help you stay present. Supervision helps you process afterward. Know your limits.

After the Session:

- Follow up with anyone who seemed distressed by the personal reflection.
- Collect Facilitator Code of Ethics if desired.
- Prepare for Chapter 6 on the circle process.

Personal Journal: Chapter 5

Date: ______________

The most important thing I learned about facilitation:

A quality I want to develop:

A wound or trigger I need to be aware of:

A skill I want to practice:

How I will care for myself in this work:

A question I'm still holding:

Key Terms Glossary for Chapter 5

Term	Definition
Phronesis	Practical wisdom; capacity to discern what a situation requires
Techne	Skill or craft knowledge
Virtue Ethics	Ethical framework focused on character, not just rules or consequences
Icon	Visible sign of invisible reality (theological term)
Compassion Fatigue	Emotional exhaustion from repeated exposure to others' suffering
Vicarious Trauma	Transformation of helper's inner experience through empathic engagement with trauma
Reintegrative Shame	Shame focused on behavior, with respect for person and pathways to repair

Term	Definition
Stigmatizing Shame	Shame focused on person as bad, leading to exclusion
Procedural Justice	Fairness of the process (voice, neutrality, respect, trust)
Cognitive Bias	Systematic pattern of deviation from rational judgment
Grounding Techniques	Practices that help regulate overwhelming emotion
Co-regulation	Regulation of emotional states through supportive interaction

"*The facilitator who embodies empathy, impartiality, patience, integrity, open-mindedness, and resilience is not merely a skilled practitioner but an icon of divine attributes.*" — Dr. Maxwell Shimba

CHAPTER 06

The Circle Process: Steps and Procedures

Learning Objectives

By completing this chapter, you will be able to:

- **Identify and explain** the six phases of the restorative justice circle process
- **Understand the purpose and function** of each phase
- **Prepare effectively** for a restorative circle
- **Facilitate each phase** with skill and sensitivity
- **Design meaningful rituals** for opening and closing circles
- **Select and use a talking piece** effectively
- **Guide groups through** storytelling, discussion, and agreement development

Key Concepts from Chapter 6

1. The Circle as Sacred Liturgy

The restorative justice circle is not merely a meeting or a conflict resolution technique. It is a sacred liturgy—a structured, ritualized enactment of the deepest truths about human relationships, accountability, and restoration. The circle embodies the conviction that:

- Justice is not something **done to** people but something **done with** people
- Healing is not **imposed** from without but **facilitated** from within
- Community is not a collection of isolated individuals but an **interdependent body**

2. The Six Phases of the Circle Process

Phase	Purpose	Key Activities
1. Preparation	Foundation for restorative encounter	Individual meetings; explaining process; addressing concerns; assessing readiness; building trust

Phase	Purpose	Key Activities
2. Opening	Creating sacred space; transition from ordinary time	Welcoming statement; purpose articulation; ritual/ceremony; ground rules; introductions
3. Sharing	Testimony of suffering and hope	Talking piece passes; each shares experience of harm and impact; no cross-talk
4. Discussion	Dialogue, understanding, and exploration	Exploring harm deeply; identifying needs; generating options; collaborative problem-solving
5. Agreement	Covenant of restoration	Summarizing discussion; identifying actions; building consensus; documenting commitments
6. Closing	Sending forth with blessing	Inviting reflections; reiterating agreements; expressing gratitude; closing ritual

3. Phase 1: Preparation – The Foundation

Theological Foundation: Preparation reflects God's way of preparing for encounter—centuries of prophecy preparing for the Messiah, John the Baptist preparing the way.

Key Elements of Preparation:

- Scheduling individual meetings with each participant
- Explaining the circle process and answering questions
- Addressing concerns and fears
- Assessing readiness (emotional, cognitive, relational)
- Clarifying roles and responsibilities
- Setting expectations (ground rules, potential outcomes)
- Building trust through active listening and personal connection

Preparation Questions for Facilitators:

- Is each participant participating voluntarily?
- Do they understand the process?
- Are they emotionally ready for direct engagement?
- What support do they need?
- Are there safety concerns?

4. Phase 2: Opening – The Portal to Sacred Space

Theological Foundation: The opening marks the threshold between ordinary time and the sacred time of the circle—like Moses at the burning ground, "Take off your sandals, for the place where you are standing is holy ground" (Exodus 3:5).

Key Elements of Opening:

- **Welcoming statement** – Warm, genuine, inclusive; expresses gratitude for presence
- **Purpose articulation** – Clear statement of why the circle is gathered
- **Ritual or ceremony** – Prayer, song, smudging, blessing, lighting a candle, moment of silence
- **Ground rules** – Speak from experience, listen without interrupting, confidentiality, respect, use of talking piece
- **Introductions/icebreakers** – Helping participants become present to one another
- **Mindfulness/centering** – Brief exercise to help participants transition

Sample Ground Rules:

- Speak from your own experience (use "I" statements)
- Listen without interrupting
- Maintain confidentiality (what's shared here stays here)
- Avoid blaming and shaming language
- Participate honestly and authentically
- The talking piece designates the speaker

5. Phase 3: Sharing – The Testimony of Suffering and Hope

Theological Foundation: The Psalms are filled with testimony—cries of lament, declarations of trust, shouts of praise. Testimony is sacred speech, articulating experiences that have been silenced.

Key Elements of Sharing:

- **Talking piece introduction** – Symbol of equal voice; only holder speaks

- **Sharing protocol** – Piece passes in order; may pass without speaking; no interruption
- **Opening invitation** – Structured but open-ended: "Share your experience of what happened, how it has affected you, and what you are hoping for"
- **Facilitator modeling** – Facilitator may speak first, modeling authentic sharing
- **Managing the round** – Maintaining structure, attending to emotions
- **Validating contributions** – Acknowledging each person's sharing
- **Managing emotional intensity** – Pausing, offering breaks, validating feelings

The Talking Piece:

- Symbolizes equal voice
- Ensures one person speaks at a time
- Creates space for focused listening
- May have symbolic significance (stone, feather, carved object)

6. Phase 4: Discussion – The Dialectic of Understanding

Theological Foundation: Discussion reflects the biblical tradition of dialogue—God with Abraham, the prophets reasoning with the people, Jesus engaging in conversation.

Key Elements of Discussion:

- **Transition from sharing** – Clearly marking shift to dialogue
- **Discussion framework** – Key questions to guide exploration

- **Open dialogue** – Encouraging participation, asking open-ended questions, summarizing, managing conflict
- **Exploring harm deeply** – Causes, consequences, meanings
- **Identifying needs** – What do victims need? Offenders? Community?
- **Brainstorming possibilities** – Creative generation of options
- **Evaluating options** – Feasibility, appropriateness, acceptability
- **Building toward consensus** – Identifying common ground, exploring trade-offs

Key Discussion Questions:

- What more do we need to understand about what happened and why?
- How has this harm affected each of us and our community?
- What do those who have been harmed need in order to heal?
- What do those who caused harm need in order to take responsibility and change?
- What resources do we have in our community to support healing?

7. Phase 5: Agreement – The Covenant of Restoration

Theological Foundation: Agreements are not merely contracts but covenants—solemn commitments to relationship, restoration, and a shared future, rooted in the biblical tradition of covenant.

Key Elements of Agreement:

- **Transition from discussion** – Moving from exploration to decision
- **Summarizing key points** – Harms, needs, options generated
- **Identifying possible actions** – Specific, achievable, relevant, measurable, time-bound
- **Evaluating options** – Feasibility, appropriateness, acceptability
- **Building consensus** – Prioritizing, sequencing, trading, testing
- **Drafting the agreement** – Clear language, specific commitments, timelines, verification
- **Documenting** – Written, signed by all participants
- **Establishing follow-up** – Check-ins, follow-up circles, progress reports

Elements of a Restorative Agreement:

- Parties involved
- Specific actions to be taken
- Timelines for completion
- Verification methods
- Consequences if commitments not fulfilled
- Follow-up arrangements

8. Phase 6: Closing – The Sending Forth

Theological Foundation: The closing is the sending forth with blessing—like Jesus sending the disciples, commissioning them to continue his mission.

Key Elements of Closing:

- **Inviting reflections** – "What is one thing you are taking away?"
- **Reiterating agreements** – Brief review of commitments
- **Facilitating expression of gratitude** – Opportunity to thank one another
- **Closing ritual** – Cultural practices, symbolic actions, shared action
- **Words of encouragement and hope** – Affirming the work done
- **Providing written reminders** – Copies of agreements
- **Clarifying follow-up arrangements** – Who, when, how
- **Formally closing the circle** – Marking the end of gathered time

Circle Flow Worksheet

Purpose: To map out each phase of a restorative circle, ensuring all elements are considered before facilitation.

Instructions: For each phase, note the key elements, questions to ask, and any specific considerations for your context.

PHASE 1: PREPARATION

Element	Your Plan / Notes
Individual meetings scheduled with:	
Process explanation to cover:	

Element	Your Plan / Notes
Concerns to address:	
Readiness assessment questions:	
Roles to clarify:	
Ground rules to discuss:	
Trust-building strategies:	

Special accommodations needed:

Preparation Checklist:

☐ All participants have been contacted
☐ Process has been explained
☐ Concerns have been addressed
☐ Readiness has been assessed
☐ Voluntary consent documented
☐ Support persons arranged (if needed)
☐ Logistics confirmed (time, place, accessibility)

PHASE 2: OPENING

Element	Your Plan / Notes
Welcoming statement (key points):	
Purpose articulation (exact language):	
Ritual/ceremony (what and why):	
Ground rules (list):	
Introduction activity:	
Mindfulness/centering practice:	

Cultural considerations:

Opening Script Outline:

PHASE 3: SHARING

Element	Your Plan / Notes
Talking piece (object and significance):	
Sharing protocol explanation:	
Opening invitation (exact words):	
Facilitator's own sharing (key points):	
Emotional support strategies:	
Validation language to use:	

Break protocol (when and how):

Opening Invitation (exact wording):

Validation Phrases:

PHASE 4: DISCUSSION

Element	Your Plan / Notes
Transition statement (from sharing):	
Key questions to guide discussion:	
Strategies for encouraging participation:	
Conflict management approaches:	

Element	Your Plan / Notes
Needs identification prompts:	
Brainstorming approach:	
Consensus-building strategies:	

Key Discussion Questions:

1. ______________________________
2. ______________________________
3. ______________________________
4. ______________________________
5. ______________________________

PHASE 5: AGREEMENT

Element	Your Plan / Notes
Transition statement (from discussion):	
Summary of key points to cover:	
Action identification criteria:	

Element	Your Plan / Notes
Consensus-testing language:	
Agreement documentation format:	
Follow-up structure:	
Consequences for non-compliance:	

Agreement Template Outline:

Follow-Up Plan:

PHASE 6: CLOSING

Element	Your Plan / Notes
Reflection prompt:	
Agreement reiteration method:	
Gratitude expression opportunity:	
Closing ritual:	
Words of encouragement:	
Written materials to distribute:	
Formal closing words:	

Closing Script:

Follow-Up Reminders to Provide:

Practical Task: Design Your Circle Elements

Purpose: To practice creating the ritual and symbolic elements of a restorative circle.

Task 1: Design an Opening Ritual

Instructions: Create an opening ritual appropriate for your context. Consider cultural sensitivity, participant backgrounds, and the purpose of the circle. Describe the ritual in detail.

Context for your ritual (school, community, workplace, faith community, etc.):

Ritual Name/Title:

Materials Needed:

Step-by-Step Description:

1.
2.
3.
4.
5.
6.

Words to be spoken (if any):

Symbolic meaning of each element:

How this ritual creates sacred space and prepares participants:

Cultural considerations/adaptations:

Task 2: Select and Describe a Talking Piece

Instructions: Choose or design a talking piece for your context. Explain its significance and how you will introduce it.

The Talking Piece (object):

Why this object? What is its significance?

Source of the object (found, made, gifted, culturally significant):

How you will introduce it to the circle (exact words):

What the talking piece symbolizes:

How you will handle the passing of the piece:

What participants should do when holding it:

What participants should do when others hold it:

_____

_____

_____

Task 3: Design a Closing Reflection

Instructions: Create a closing reflection activity that helps participants integrate their experience and transition back to ordinary life.

Closing Reflection Activity:

_____

Purpose of this activity:

_____

Time needed: ______________

Materials needed: ______________

Step-by-Step Instructions:

1. _____
2. _____
3. _____

4. ____________________
5. ____________________

Facilitator Script:

____

____

____

How this activity provides closure:

____

____

How it helps participants carry the circle forward:

____

____

____

Exercise 1: Preparation Scenarios

Purpose: To practice handling common preparation challenges.

Instructions: For each scenario, describe how you would respond.

Scenario 1: The Fearful Victim

A victim says in preparation: "I want to do this, but I'm terrified. What if I see him and I can't speak? What if I get angry and say things I regret? What if he denies everything?"

Your response:

Scenario 2: The Resistant Offender

An offender says: "I don't see the point. I already apologized. The court said I have to do this, so I'll do it, but I don't see what good it will do."

Your response:

Scenario 3: The Overprotective Parent

A parent of a young offender says: "My child has been through enough. I don't want them traumatized by having to face this victim. This isn't fair."

Your response:

Scenario 4: The Skeptical Community Member

A community member invited to participate says: "Why should I give up my evening for this? I didn't do anything wrong. This is between them."

Your response:

Exercise 2: Sharing Phase Practice

Purpose: To practice facilitating the sharing phase with different types of participants.

Instructions: For each participant type, write what you would say to:

- Invite them to share
- Validate their contribution
- Support them if they become emotional

Participant Type	Invitation	Validation	Emotional Support
A tearful victim			
An angry victim			

Participant Type	Invitation	Validation	Emotional Support
A remorseful offender			
A defensive offender			
A silent community member			
A talkative community member			

Exercise 3: Discussion Phase Scenarios

Purpose: To practice facilitating discussion through challenging moments.

Instructions: For each scenario, write what you would say or do as facilitator.

Scenario 1: The Discussion Goes in Circles

The group has been discussing the same point for 20 minutes. No new insights are emerging. People are getting frustrated.

Your intervention:

Scenario 2: Participants Disagree Strongly

Two participants have very different accounts of what happened. They are starting to argue, each insisting they are right.

Your intervention:

Scenario 3: Someone Makes an Unrealistic Suggestion

An offender suggests community service they cannot physically perform. Others seem hesitant to challenge it.

Your intervention:

Scenario 4: The Group Can't Agree

The group has been trying to reach consensus for 30 minutes. Several options have been discussed, but there is no agreement. People are getting tired.

Your intervention:

Exercise 4: Agreement Drafting

Purpose: To practice drafting clear, specific restorative agreements.

Scenario:

A teenager, Jamal (16), vandalized a neighbor's fence, causing $500 in damage. The neighbor, Mrs. Washington, is elderly and lives alone. She was frightened and feels violated. Jamal has expressed remorse and wants to make things right. His mother is a single parent working two jobs. Mrs. Washington's son is concerned about his mother's safety.

Instructions: Draft a complete restorative agreement based on this scenario.

Agreement:

Date: ______________

Participants:

- Jamal (offender)
- Mrs. Washington (victim)
- Jamal's mother
- Mrs. Washington's son
- Facilitator

Harm Addressed:

Acknowledgment of Responsibility:

Agreed Actions:

Action	Responsible Party	Deadline	Verification

Support Commitments:

Follow-Up Plan:

Signatures:

__________________________ (Jamal)

__________________________ (Mrs. Washington)

__________________________ (Facilitator)

________________________ (Date)

Circle Practice: Full Circle Simulation

Purpose: To practice facilitating all six phases of a circle in a simulated setting.

Time: 60–90 minutes

Format: Small groups of 6-8 people. One person serves as facilitator. Others play roles based on a scenario. After the circle, debrief thoroughly.

Scenario for Simulation:

A workplace conflict: Two colleagues, Maria and James, have been in conflict for months. Maria feels James takes credit for her work and undermines her in meetings. James feels Maria is overly sensitive and refuses to collaborate. Their conflict is affecting team morale and productivity. Human resources has referred them to a restorative circle.

Roles:

- **Maria** – Feels wronged, angry, wants acknowledgment
- **James** – Feels misunderstood, defensive, wants to move on
- **Team Leader** – Concerned about team morale, wants resolution
- **HR Representative** – Observing, will need to document outcome

- **Support Person for Maria** – A colleague who can support her
- **Support Person for James** – A colleague who can support him
- **Facilitator** – Guides the entire process

Instructions for Facilitator:

1. **Preparation** (do this before the circle, even in simulation): Meet individually with each participant (brief 2-3 minute check-ins) to explain the process and assess readiness.
2. **Opening** (5-7 minutes): Welcome, purpose, ground rules, introductions, brief centering.
3. **Sharing** (15-20 minutes): Talking piece passes; each shares their experience of the conflict and its impact.
4. **Discussion** (15-20 minutes): Facilitate dialogue exploring causes, needs, and possible solutions.
5. **Agreement** (10-15 minutes): Help participants develop specific commitments.
6. **Closing** (5 minutes): Reflections, gratitude, formal closing.

Debrief Questions:

For the facilitator:

- What felt natural?
- What was challenging?
- How did you decide when to intervene?
- What would you do differently?

For participants:

- How did the facilitator's presence affect the process?
- What did the facilitator do that was helpful?
- What could have been done differently?

For observers:

- What did you notice about the facilitator's interventions?
- How did the process unfold?

Practical Assignment: Observe or Facilitate a Circle

Purpose: To gain real experience with the circle process.

Instructions:

1. **If possible, observe** an actual restorative justice circle. If not, observe a simulation or watch a video recording of a restorative circle.
2. **Take detailed notes** using the Circle Observation Form below.
3. **Write a 2-3 page reflection** addressing:
   - What you observed in each phase
   - What the facilitator did well
   - What challenges arose and how they were handled
   - What you learned about the circle process
   - How you will apply this learning to your own facilitation

Circle Observation Form

Date of Circle: ______________

Context: ____

Facilitator(s): ____

Number of Participants: ______________

Phase	What Happened	Facilitator Actions	Your Observations
Preparation (if known)			
Opening			
Sharing			
Discussion			

Agreement

Closing

Overall Observations:

What did the facilitator do well?

What challenges arose? How were they handled?

What surprised you?

What will you carry into your own facilitation?

Reflection Questions

1. Which phase of the circle process do you think will be most challenging for you? Why?

2. Which phase do you most look forward to facilitating? Why?

3. The chapter describes the circle as "sacred liturgy." How does this understanding affect how you approach each phase?

4. How will you ensure that the circle remains safe for all participants throughout the process?

5. What role does silence play in the circle? How will you honor silence?

6. How will you know when a phase is complete and it's time to move to the next?

7. What support do you need to facilitate circles with confidence and skill?

Facilitator Notes for Chapter 6

Before the Session:

1. **Read Chapter 6 thoroughly.** The circle process is the heart of restorative practice. Ensure you understand each phase deeply.
2. **Prepare for the full circle simulation.** This is the most complex exercise. You may want to brief role-players in advance and allow adequate time.
3. **Gather talking piece examples.** Bring several objects that could serve as talking pieces and explain their significance.
4. **Prepare ritual materials.** If designing opening rituals, have art supplies, candles, fabric, or other materials available.

Session Outline (3.5–4 hours):

Segment	Time	Activity
Opening	10 min	Welcome, check-in, review objectives
Key Concepts	25 min	Present six phases of circle process
Circle Flow Worksheet	20 min	Individual work on worksheet
Design Opening Ritual	15 min	Small group design work

Segment	Time	Activity
Share Rituals	10 min	Groups share their rituals
Talking Piece Discussion	10 min	Share and discuss talking pieces
Preparation Scenarios	15 min	Small group discussion
Break	10 min	
Full Circle Simulation	75 min	Set-up, circle, debrief
Debrief Simulation	15 min	Large group share
Agreement Drafting	15 min	Practice drafting agreements

Segment	Time	Activity
Reflection Questions	10 min	Individual writing
Closing	5 min	Review assignment, closing words

Key Teaching Points:

1. **Each phase has a purpose.** Skipping or rushing phases undermines the circle's work. Preparation is as important as the circle itself.
2. **The facilitator's role changes across phases.** In sharing, you guard the structure; in discussion, you facilitate dialogue; in agreement, you guide decision-making.
3. **The talking piece is sacred.** It embodies equal voice and ensures deep listening. Honor it.
4. **Ritual matters.** Opening and closing rituals create the container that holds the difficult work of sharing and discussion.
5. **Agreements must be specific.** Vague agreements fail. Push for clarity: who, what, when, how, verification.
6. **The circle is not therapy, but it is therapeutic.** The goal is not treatment but restoration, which has healing effects.

Common Questions:

- **Q: "What if someone refuses to use the talking piece?"**
A: Explain its purpose again. If they still refuse, they may not be ready for circle. Consider more preparation.
- **Q: "How long should each phase take?"**
A: There's no fixed time. Let the process unfold. Some circles take 2 hours, some take 6. Rushing is worse than length.
- **Q: "What if we run out of time?"**
A: Better to continue another day than to rush the end. Schedule follow-up sessions if needed.
- **Q: "Can we skip the opening ritual if participants are uncomfortable with it?"**
A: Adapt, don't abandon. Find a ritual that works for everyone—a moment of silence, a breathing exercise, a simple welcome.
- **Q: "What if no agreement is reached?"**
A: Sometimes agreement isn't possible. Document what was accomplished and what remains. The process still had value.

After the Session:

- Collect observation forms if used.
- Follow up with anyone who facilitated the simulation for additional feedback.
- Prepare for Chapter 7 on case studies.

Personal Journal: Chapter 6

Date: ______________

The most important thing I learned about the circle process:

A phase I want to practice more:

A ritual I want to create or learn:

A talking piece I would choose and why:

What I'm learning about myself as a facilitator:

A question I'm still holding:

Key Terms Glossary for Chapter 6

Term	Definition
Liturgy	Structured, ritualized enactment of shared meaning and values
Preparation Phase	Individual meetings before circle to build foundation
Opening Phase	Ritual transition creating sacred space for circle

Term	Definition
Sharing Phase	Testimony of experiences using talking piece
Discussion Phase	Dialogue exploring harm, needs, and possibilities
Agreement Phase	Collaborative development of restorative commitments
Closing Phase	Ritual sending forth with blessing and hope
Talking Piece	Object passed around circle; only holder speaks
Ground Rules	Shared expectations for respectful participation
Sacred Space	Space set apart for transformative work

Term	Definition
Liminality	"Betwixt and between" state where transformation becomes possible
Covenant	Solemn commitment to relationship, distinguished from contract
Kairos	Opportune time, sacred time, distinguished from chronos (clock time)

"The six phases of the circle process constitute a complete liturgical cycle. They move participants from the isolation of individual experience through the vulnerability of shared testimony and the challenge of collective deliberation to the hope of restored relationship." — Dr. Maxwell Shimba

CHAPTER 07

Case Studies: Success Stories from Restorative Justice Circles

Learning Objectives

By completing this chapter, you will be able to:

- **Analyze real-world restorative justice cases** using a structured framework
- **Identify the key elements** that made restoration possible in diverse contexts
- **Understand the impact** of restorative justice on victims, offenders, and communities
- **Compare restorative approaches** across different settings (schools, communities, workplaces)
- **Apply lessons** from case studies to your own context

- **Discern the spiritual and psychological dimensions** of restorative transformation

---

Key Concepts from Chapter 7

1. Case Studies as Sacred Testimony

The case studies in this chapter are not merely illustrative examples or anecdotal evidence. They are **sacred testimonies**—witness accounts of transformation that bear witness to the power of restorative processes to heal wounds, restore relationships, and rebuild communities. Each case study is a narrative of grace, a story of how the restorative cycles woven into the fabric of creation can be activated through faithful practice.

2. The Three Case Studies

Case Study	Setting	Harm	Restorative Response	Outcome
Case Study 1	Middle School	Bullying of a new student	Circle with victim, offenders, affected students	Decreased bullying; improved school climate

Case Study	Setting	Harm	Restorative Response	Outcome
Case Study 2	Neighborhood	Vandalism damaging property and community trust	Circle with residents, offenders, community leaders	Restored property; youth programs; neighborhood watch
Case Study 3	Workplace	Conflicts creating toxic environment	Circles for conflict resolution, communication, team-building	Improved relationships; increased productivity

3. Common Elements Across Case Studies

Element	Description
Thorough Preparation	Individual meetings built trust and readiness

Element	Description
Inclusive Participation	All affected parties were present
Structured Process	Clear phases (opening, sharing, discussion, agreement, closing)
Skilled Facilitation	Trained facilitators guided the process
Collaborative Agreements	Participants developed solutions together
Ongoing Follow-Up	Circles reconvened to monitor progress

4. The Restorative Cycles in Case Studies

Cycle Phase	Case Study Manifestation
Inflammatory Phase (acknowledgment of harm)	Sharing stories of impact; victims naming suffering; offenders hearing consequences

Cycle Phase	Case Study Manifestation
Proliferative Phase (active reconstruction)	Discussion exploring causes; brainstorming solutions; developing agreements
Remodeling Phase (strengthening and integration)	Implementation of agreements; follow-up meetings; sustained change

5. Theological Dimensions

Case Study	Theological Themes
School-Based	"The least of these" (Matthew 25); body of Christ suffering together; lost sheep (Luke 15)
Community-Based	Shalom (comprehensive peace); covenant renewal; Jubilee restoration
Workplace-Based	Vocation as calling; body of Christ at work; confession and restoration

6. Psychological Dimensions

Benefit	Description
Empathy Development	Offenders heard victims' experiences firsthand
Validation	Victims felt heard and believed
Closure	Victims received acknowledgment and answers
Reintegrative Shame	Offenders experienced shame focused on behavior, not identity
Collective Efficacy	Communities developed belief in their capacity to solve problems

---

Case Analysis Template

Purpose: To provide a consistent framework for analyzing any restorative justice case.

Instructions: For each case study you read or observe, complete this template.

CASE ANALYSIS: ___________________________

Date of Analysis: _______________

1. THE HARM

Question	Your Analysis
What was the harm? (Describe the incident or situation)	
Who committed the harm? (Offender information - age, relationship, context)	
What was the immediate impact?	
What were the ripple effects? (Who else was affected?)	

Question	Your Analysis
What underlying issues contributed to the harm?	

2. THOSE AFFECTED

Question	Your Analysis
Who was the direct victim? How were they affected?	
Who else was affected? (Family, friends, witnesses, community)	
How was the community affected? (Trust, safety, cohesion)	
What did each stakeholder need for healing?	
Who was included in the restorative process?	

3. ACCOUNTABILITY

Question	Your Analysis
How did the offender acknowledge responsibility?	
Was the acknowledgment genuine or coerced? Evidence?	
What did the offender learn or understand through the process?	
How did the offender demonstrate remorse?	
What actions did the offender take to make amends?	

4. RESTORATION

Question	Your Analysis
What material reparation occurred? (Restitution, service, etc.)	

Question	Your Analysis
What emotional or relational repair occurred?	
How was the victim's voice honored?	
How was the community involved in restoration?	
What agreements were made? (Specific actions, timelines)	
How was the offender reintegrated into community?	
What follow-up occurred?	

5. OUTCOMES

Question	Your Analysis
What changed for the victim?	

Question	Your Analysis
What changed for the offender?	
What changed for the community?	
Were agreements fulfilled? Evidence?	
Were there any unintended outcomes (positive or negative)?	
What was sustained over time?	

6. WHAT MADE RESTORATION POSSIBLE?

Factor	How It Contributed
Preparation	
Facilitation	
Participant willingness	

Factor	How It Contributed
Community support	
Institutional backing	
Cultural appropriateness	
Time and space	
Other factors	

7. LESSONS LEARNED

What lessons from this case can be applied to other contexts?

What challenges emerged and how were they addressed?

What would you have done differently?

CASE STUDY 1: School-Based Restorative Justice Circle

Background:

A middle school was experiencing ongoing bullying incidents, creating a hostile environment for several students. Traditional disciplinary measures—detention, suspension, parent conferences—had not resolved the issue or supported the victims. The school decided to implement restorative justice circles to address specific bullying incidents.

The Incident:

Emily, a new student, had been targeted by a group of students for several weeks. The bullying included mocking, exclusion, and online harassment. Emily had become withdrawn, was missing school, and her grades were falling. The school had suspended the offenders, but the bullying continued and Emily remained fearful.

The Restorative Process:

- Facilitators held individual preparation meetings with Emily, the offenders, and other students affected by the bullying.
- A restorative justice circle was convened including Emily, the offenders, several other students who had witnessed or been affected by the bullying, teachers, and a facilitator.
- During the circle, Emily shared her experience of the bullying and its impact on her life. Offenders shared their perspectives and, over the course of the circle, began to understand the harm they had caused.
- Other students described how the bullying had affected the school environment and their own sense of safety.
- The group collaboratively developed agreements: formal apologies from the offenders, participation in anti-bullying workshops, and establishment of a peer support program.

- Follow-up circles were held to monitor progress and ensure agreements were kept.

Outcomes:

- Emily reported feeling heard and supported. Her attendance and grades improved.
- Offenders gained deeper understanding of the impact of their actions and took responsibility.
- Anti-bullying workshops educated students about the effects of bullying.
- The peer support program created ongoing structures for support and accountability.
- Follow-up meetings confirmed sustained improvements in behavior and relationships.

Case Analysis: School-Based Circle

Complete the template for Case Study 1:

1. THE HARM

What was the harm?

Who committed the harm?

What was the immediate impact?

What were the ripple effects?

What underlying issues may have contributed?

2. THOSE AFFECTED

Who was the direct victim? How were they affected?

Who else was affected?

How was the community (school) affected?

What did each stakeholder need for healing?

Who was included in the restorative process?

3. ACCOUNTABILITY

How did the offenders acknowledge responsibility?

Was the acknowledgment genuine? Evidence?

What did the offenders learn or understand?

How did they demonstrate remorse?

What actions did they take to make amends?

4. RESTORATION

What material reparation occurred?

What emotional or relational repair occurred?

How was Emily's voice honored?

How was the school community involved?

What agreements were made?

How were offenders reintegrated?

What follow-up occurred?

5. OUTCOMES

What changed for Emily?

What changed for the offenders?

What changed for the school community?

Were agreements fulfilled?

What was sustained over time?

6. WHAT MADE RESTORATION POSSIBLE?

Factor	How It Contributed
Preparation	
Facilitation	
Participant willingness	
School support	
Inclusion of peers	
Follow-up structure	

7. LESSONS LEARNED

What lessons from this case apply to other schools?

What challenges might arise in similar cases?

CASE STUDY 2: Community Restorative Justice Circle

Background:

A neighborhood was struggling with repeated vandalism. Over several months, someone had been spray-painting graffiti on buildings, breaking streetlights, and damaging public property. Residents felt unsafe, angry, and disconnected from one another. Trust in the community was eroding.

The Incident:

Three teenagers were identified as responsible for much of the vandalism. They had been caught on security cameras and identified by neighbors. The police were involved, but residents wanted more than punishment—they wanted the damage repaired, the behavior to stop, and their community to heal.

The Restorative Process:

- Facilitators held individual meetings with affected residents, the teenagers and their families, and community leaders.
- A restorative justice circle was convened including residents whose property was damaged, the teenagers and their parents, community leaders, a local business owner, and a facilitator.

- Residents shared how the vandalism had affected them—not only the property damage but the fear, the anger, the sense that their community was no longer safe.
- The teenagers explained their motivations—boredom, peer pressure, lack of constructive activities. They heard, perhaps for the first time, the real impact of their actions.
- Community members discussed the broader impact on neighborhood cohesion and safety. They also acknowledged that the community had failed to provide positive opportunities for youth.
- The group collaboratively developed solutions: the teenagers would participate in community cleanup events, help repair damaged property, and contribute to creating a youth recreational program. A neighborhood watch was established to improve safety and build connections among residents.
- Regular follow-up circles were scheduled to monitor progress and continue community-building.

Outcomes:

- The physical appearance of the neighborhood was restored.
- Residents reported enhanced pride and ownership.
- Youth recreational programs provided constructive activities, reducing future vandalism.
- The neighborhood watch improved safety and built connections among residents.
- Follow-up meetings demonstrated sustained engagement and continued efforts to build a cohesive community.

Case Analysis: Community-Based Circle

Complete the template for Case Study 2:

1. THE HARM

What was the harm?

Who committed the harm?

What was the immediate impact?

What were the ripple effects?

What underlying issues may have contributed?

2. THOSE AFFECTED

Who were the direct victims? How were they affected?

Who else was affected?

How was the community affected?

What did each stakeholder need for healing?

Who was included in the restorative process?

3. ACCOUNTABILITY

How did the teenagers acknowledge responsibility?

Was the acknowledgment genuine? Evidence?

What did they learn or understand?

How did they demonstrate remorse?

What actions did they take to make amends?

4. RESTORATION

What material reparation occurred?

What emotional or relational repair occurred?

How were victims' voices honored?

How was the community involved?

What agreements were made?

How were the teenagers reintegrated?

What follow-up occurred?

5. OUTCOMES

What changed for the victims?

What changed for the teenagers?

What changed for the community?

Were agreements fulfilled?

What was sustained over time?

---

6. WHAT MADE RESTORATION POSSIBLE?

Factor	How It Contributed
Preparation	
Facilitation	
Community involvement	
Youth engagement	
Addressing root causes	
Ongoing structure	

7. LESSONS LEARNED

What lessons from this case apply to other communities?

What challenges might arise in similar cases?

CASE STUDY 3: Workplace Restorative Justice Circle

Background:

A mid-sized company faced ongoing conflicts between two departments—sales and operations. Sales accused operations of being unresponsive and inflexible; operations accused sales of making unrealistic promises and failing to communicate. The conflict had escalated over months, creating a hostile work environment and decreasing productivity.

The Restorative Process:

- Facilitators held individual preparation meetings with employees from both departments, including managers and front-line staff.

- Conflict resolution circles were implemented, bringing together employees from both departments.
- During circles, employees shared their experiences and the impact of conflicts on their work and well-being. They were encouraged to understand each other's perspectives and take responsibility for their actions.
- The circles explored underlying issues: communication breakdowns, workload stress, lack of team cohesion.
- Agreements were developed for improved communication protocols, joint team-building activities, and regular check-ins to monitor progress.
- Follow-up circles were conducted to review progress and address ongoing challenges.

Outcomes:

- The frequency and intensity of conflicts decreased significantly.
- Employees reported feeling heard, validated, and more connected to colleagues.
- Team-building activities and improved communication fostered a more collaborative environment.
- Stress management resources were provided, reducing workplace stress and improving well-being.
- Follow-up meetings confirmed sustained improvements in workplace relationships and productivity.

Case Analysis: Workplace-Based Circle

Complete the template for Case Study 3:

1. THE HARM

What was the harm?

Who was involved in the conflict?

What was the immediate impact?

What were the ripple effects?

What underlying issues contributed?

---

2. THOSE AFFECTED

Who were the direct parties? How were they affected?

Who else was affected?

How was the organization affected?

What did each stakeholder need for healing?

Who was included in the restorative process?

3. ACCOUNTABILITY

How did employees take responsibility?

Was the acknowledgment genuine? Evidence?

What did they learn or understand?

How did they demonstrate commitment to change?

What actions did they take to make amends?

4. RESTORATION

What material changes occurred?

What emotional or relational repair occurred?

How were voices honored?

How was the organization involved?

What agreements were made?

How was collaboration rebuilt?

What follow-up occurred?

5. OUTCOMES

What changed for employees?

What changed for managers?

What changed for the organization?

Were agreements fulfilled?

What was sustained over time?

6. WHAT MADE RESTORATION POSSIBLE?

Factor	How It Contributed
Preparation	
Facilitation	
Management support	
Employee participation	
Addressing systemic issues	
Follow-up structure	

7. LESSONS LEARNED

What lessons from this case apply to other workplaces?

What challenges might arise in similar cases?

Comparative Analysis: All Three Cases

Instructions: After analyzing each case individually, compare them using this table.

Element	School Case	Community Case	Workplace Case
Type of Harm			
Victim(s)			
Offender(s)			

Element	School Case	Community Case	Workplace Case
Community Affected			
Preparation Approach			
Key Facilitator Actions			
Emotional Dynamics			
Agreements Made			
Restorative Actions			
Follow-Up			
Outcomes			

Element	School Case	Community Case	Workplace Case
Challenges Faced			

Comparative Reflection Questions:

1. What common elements do you see across all three cases?

2. What differences stand out? What accounts for these differences?

3. Which case resonated most with you? Why?

4. What principles of restorative justice were demonstrated in all three?

5. What role did community play in each case? How did that differ?

6. What role did follow-up play in sustaining outcomes?

7. If you were to design a restorative response for a similar situation in your context, what would you borrow from these cases?

Group Discussion Questions

Purpose: To facilitate rich discussion of the case studies in a group setting.

Instructions: Use these questions to guide small group or large group discussion.

---

1. What made restoration possible in each case?

Consider:

- Preparation
- Facilitation
- Participant willingness
- Community involvement
- Institutional support
- Time and space
- Follow-up

School Case:

Community Case:

Workplace Case:

Common factors across cases:

2. What role did the facilitator play in each case?

Case	Facilitator Actions	Impact
School		
Community		

Case	Facilitator Actions	Impact
Workplace		

What qualities and skills did facilitators demonstrate?

---

3. How did victims experience healing in each case?

Case	What victims needed	How circle provided it
School (Emily)		
Community (residents)		
Workplace (employees)		

What does this teach about victim healing?

4. How did offenders experience accountability in each case?

Case	Offender's initial state	What changed	How
School (bullies)			
Community (teens)			
Workplace (both sides)			

What does this teach about genuine accountability?

5. How did community involvement strengthen each process?

Case	Who from community participated	What they contributed
School		
Community		
Workplace		

What happens when community is excluded?

6. What challenges emerged in each case and how were they addressed?

Case	Challenge	Response	Was it effective?
School			
Community			
Workplace			

What does this teach about navigating challenges?

7. What would you have done differently in any of these cases?

8. What lessons do indigenous justice systems offer modern societies?

Drawing on Chapter 3 and these case studies, consider:

- What elements of indigenous restorative traditions (Māori, First Nations, Ubuntu) are reflected in these cases?
- What might these cases have looked like if they had more fully incorporated indigenous wisdom?
- How can modern restorative practice learn from indigenous approaches to:
    - The role of elders?
    - Spiritual elements?
    - Community involvement?
    - Holistic healing?
    - Interconnectedness?

Exercise 1: Identifying Restorative Principles in Action

Purpose: To connect the six core principles to concrete case examples.

Instructions: For each principle, identify at least one example from the case studies where that principle was demonstrated.

Principle	Example from Case Studies
Inclusivity (all affected parties present)	
Voluntariness (free participation)	
Respect and Equality (all voices valued)	
Accountability (active responsibility)	
Reparation (tangible repair)	

Principle	Example from Case Studies
Reintegration (welcome back to community)	

Exercise 2: Restorative Cycles Analysis

Purpose: To identify the three phases of restorative cycles in each case.

Instructions: For each case, identify what represented each phase.

Phase	School Case	Community Case	Workplace Case
Inflammatory Phase (acknowledgment of harm)			

Phase	School Case	Com-munity Case	Work-place Case
Proliferative Phase (active reconstruction)			
Remodeling Phase (strengthening and integration)			

Exercise 3: What If? Scenario Variations

Purpose: To explore how cases might change under different circumstances.

Instructions: For each case, consider the "what if" scenario and discuss how the process and outcome might differ.

School Case "What If":

What if Emily had not been willing to participate? How might the process change?

What if the offenders had denied responsibility throughout?

What if parents had refused to allow their children to participate?

Community Case "What If":

What if the teenagers had been adults with long criminal histories?

What if the property damage had been much more severe?

What if some residents refused to participate and demanded punishment instead?

Workplace Case "What If":

What if the conflict involved harassment based on protected characteristics?

What if the CEO was part of the problem and refused to participate?

What if the conflict had gone on for years and involved litigation?

Exercise 4: Designing a Follow-Up Circle

Purpose: To practice planning the crucial follow-up phase.

Instructions: Choose one of the three cases. Design a follow-up circle to occur six months after the initial circle.

Case Selected: ______________________________

Purpose of Follow-Up Circle:

Who Should Attend:

Preparation Needed:

Opening Ritual:

Key Questions to Ask:

1.
2.
3.
4.

How to Address Challenges (if agreements weren't kept):

How to Celebrate Successes (if agreements were kept):

Closing Ritual:

Circle Practice: "A Story of Restoration I Have Witnessed"

Purpose: To connect personal experience with the themes of the case studies.

Time: 45–60 minutes

Materials: Talking piece, comfortable seating

Opening (5 minutes):

- Welcome participants.
- Remind of confidentiality.
- Introduce the prompt: "Share a story of restoration you have witnessed—a time when harm was acknowledged, accountability occurred, and healing began. This could be from your own life, your family, your community, or something you have observed."

Check-In Round (10 minutes):

- Pass the talking piece. Each person shares their name and one word about how they're arriving.

Sharing Round (20–30 minutes):

- Pass the talking piece. Each person who wishes responds to the prompt.
- Allow silence between speakers.

- No cross-talk or response.

Reflection Round (10 minutes):

- Pass the talking piece. Each person shares: "What did I learn from hearing these stories of restoration?"

Closing (5 minutes):

- Thank participants.
- Note the themes of hope and healing that emerged.
- Close with a moment of silence.

Practical Assignment: Document a Local Case

Purpose: To apply case analysis skills to a real situation in your own context.

Instructions:

1. Identify a situation in your community, school, workplace, or organization where restorative justice was used (or could have been used) to address harm.
2. Gather as much information as possible through observation, interviews, or documentation.
3. Complete the Case Analysis Template for this situation.
4. Write a 2-3 page reflection addressing:
    - What made restoration possible (or what prevented it)?

- How does this case compare to the three cases in this chapter?
- What lessons can be learned for future restorative work?
- What would you have done differently?

Confidentiality Note: Change names and identifying details to protect privacy.

Reflection Questions

1. Which of the three cases affected you most emotionally? Why?

2. In which case do you think restoration was most complete? What criteria are you using?

3. The chapter describes case studies as "sacred testimonies." What does this mean to you? How does it affect how you read these stories?

4. What surprised you about these cases?

5. What questions do you still have about what happened in these cases?

6. If you could ask one question to a participant in each case, what would you ask?
   - To Emily (school case): ______________________________
   - To a resident (community case): ______________________________
   - To an employee (workplace case): ______________________________
7. How do these cases give you hope about the possibility of restoration in difficult situations?

8. What caution do these cases offer? What could go wrong?

Facilitator Notes for Chapter 7

Before the Session:

1. **Read Chapter 7 thoroughly.** Familiarize yourself with all three case studies and the analysis framework.
2. **Prepare case materials.** Have copies of the case studies and analysis templates for all participants.
3. **Consider video/audio supplements.** If available, find recordings of restorative justice circles or interviews with participants to supplement the written cases.
4. **Prepare for emotional responses.** These cases involve real harm and real healing. Participants may have strong emotional reactions.

Session Outline (2.5–3 hours):

Segment	Time	Activity
Opening	10 min	Welcome, check-in, review objectives
Key Concepts	15 min	Review case study framework and restorative cycles
Case Study 1 Analysis	30 min	Read and analyze school case (small groups)
Case Study 2 Analysis	30 min	Read and analyze community case (small groups)
Break	10 min	
Case Study 3 Analysis	30 min	Read and analyze workplace case (small groups)
Comparative Discussion	20 min	Large group discussion of all three cases

Segment	Time	Activity
Circle Practice	20 min	"A Story of Restoration I Have Witnessed"
Assignment Review	5 min	Explain local case documentation assignment
Closing	5 min	Final reflections, closing words

Alternative Format (if time is limited):

Assign different cases to different small groups. Each group analyzes their case and presents findings to the large group. Then conduct comparative discussion.

Key Teaching Points:

1. **Case studies are not just illustrations.** They are sources of deep learning about what makes restorative justice work.
2. **Context matters.** Each case succeeded because it was adapted to its specific context—school, community, workplace.
3. **Preparation and follow-up are essential.** These cases show that the circle itself is only part of the story.

4. **Restoration is possible even in serious harm.** These cases involved significant harm, yet restoration occurred.
5. **Success is not guaranteed.** These are success stories, but they required hard work, skilled facilitation, and participant willingness.

Common Questions:

- **Q: "Are these cases real?"**
  A: They are based on real restorative justice cases, with details adapted for teaching.
- **Q: "What about cases where restorative justice fails?"**
  A: Those are important too. Chapter 8 addresses challenges and failures.
- **Q: "How can I find cases from my own community?"**
  A: Contact local restorative justice programs, courts, schools, or community organizations. Many are willing to share stories (with confidentiality).
- **Q: "Can I share my own case?"**
  A: Yes, if you protect confidentiality. The practical assignment invites this.

After the Session:

- Collect case analyses if desired.
- Follow up on local case documentation assignment.
- Prepare for Chapter 8 on challenges and solutions.

Personal Journal: Chapter 7

Date: _______________

The case that most moved me:

What I learned about what makes restoration possible:

A question these cases raised for me:

How these cases connect to my context:

A hope I'm carrying forward:

Key Terms Glossary for Chapter 7

Term	Definition
Case Study	In-depth examination of a real-world example
Testimony	Sacred speech bearing witness to transformation
Restorative Cycles	Inflammatory, proliferative, and remodeling phases of healing
Collective Efficacy	Shared belief that community can solve problems together
Reintegrative Shame	Shame focused on behavior, with respect for person

Term	Definition
Procedural Justice	Fairness of the process (voice, neutrality, respect, trust)
Social Capital	Networks of relationships, trust, and reciprocity
Post-Traumatic Growth	Positive psychological change after trauma
Closure	Sense of completion that enables moving forward
Follow-Up	Ongoing engagement after the initial circle

"These three case studies are testimonies to the transformative power of restorative justice circles. Each demonstrates how the principles and practices examined throughout this book can be enacted in real situations with real people, producing outcomes that are not merely satisfactory but transformative." — Dr. Maxwell Shimba

CHAPTER 08

Challenges and Solutions in Restorative Justice Circles

Learning Objectives

By completing this chapter, you will be able to:

- **Identify the five common challenges** that arise in restorative justice circles
- **Understand the theological, psychological, and practical dimensions** of each challenge
- **Develop preventive strategies** to minimize the likelihood of challenges
- **Design intervention strategies** to address challenges when they occur

- **Apply restorative principles** to the challenges themselves
- **Build resilience** as a facilitator and community to navigate difficulties

Key Concepts from Chapter 8

1. The Refining Fire of Restorative Practice

The challenges that arise in restorative justice circles are not evidence of failure but evidence of fidelity. They are:

- **Growing pains** of communities learning to address harm differently
- **Birth pangs** of new relationships struggling to be born
- **Refining fire** that tests and strengthens restorative practice

The same God who tested Abraham, wrestled with Jacob, and led Israel through the wilderness permits challenges not to defeat practitioners but to refine them, not to destroy circles but to strengthen them.

2. The Five Common Challenges

Challenge	Description
Resistance	Reluctance to participate; denial of responsibility; skepticism about process

Challenge	Description
Cultural Barriers	Differences in communication styles, values, expectations, and language
Emotional Intensity	Overwhelming anger, sadness, shame, or fear that disrupts process
Power Imbalances	Differences in status, authority, confidence, or resources that affect participation
Logistical Issues	Scheduling conflicts, resource limitations, venue accessibility

3. Challenge 1: Resistance

Theological Foundation: God respects human freedom, even when exercised in resistance. The father waits for the prodigal; he does not pursue or compel. Resistance is not merely an obstacle but an expression of human freedom to be respected.

Psychological Dimensions:

- **Fear** – of facing those harmed, of shame, of consequences
- **Mistrust** – based on past experiences with institutions
- **Skepticism** – doubt that process can help
- **Denial** – psychological protection from shame

- **Reactance** – intensified resistance when freedom feels threatened

Legal Framework:

- Voluntariness requires free consent; coercion invalidates process
- Right to withdraw at any time must be honored
- Informed consent requires understanding of process and consequences

Restorative Cycles Parallel: Resistance is like the body's protective immune response—a defense mechanism that must be respected and carefully engaged, not simply overridden.

Preventive Strategies:

- Build trust through thorough preparation
- Provide clear education about process
- Emphasize voluntary nature repeatedly
- Use peer support and testimony from past participants
- Individualize preparation to address specific concerns

Intervention Strategies:

- Listen to concerns without defensiveness
- Validate fears while offering reassurance
- Re-emphasize choice and control
- Offer additional preparation time
- Consider postponing if resistance is too high

---

4. Challenge 2: Cultural Barriers

Theological Foundation: Pentecost reverses Babel—diversity is not erased but redeemed through mutual understanding across difference. The early church's inclusion of Gentiles models faithful engagement with cultural difference.

Psychological Dimensions:

- **Cultural identity** affects how participants perceive themselves and others
- **Communication styles** vary (direct/indirect, emotional/reserved)
- **Individualism vs. collectivism** affects understanding of responsibility
- **Power distance** affects willingness to speak freely

Legal Framework:

- Cultural rights recognized in international law
- Non-discrimination principles require equal access
- Language access may be legally required (interpreters, translated materials)

Restorative Cycles Parallel: Cultural diversity is like biodiversity in ecosystems—it enhances resilience, creativity, and adaptive capacity when honored, but causes friction when ignored.

Preventive Strategies:

- Cultural sensitivity training for facilitators
- Learn about participants' cultural backgrounds
- Engage cultural leaders and elders
- Prepare translated materials and interpreters
- Design inclusive practices from the start

Intervention Strategies:

- Acknowledge cultural differences openly and respectfully
- Ask participants about their preferences and needs
- Adapt processes in real-time when possible
- Bring in cultural consultants if needed
- Apologize and learn from mistakes

---

5. Challenge 3: Emotional Intensity

Theological Foundation: The Psalms are filled with raw emotion—anger, fear, despair, hope. God is not threatened by human emotion. Jesus wept, was angry, and cried out in agony. Emotional intensity is not a sign that something is wrong but that something real is happening.

Psychological Dimensions:

- **Emotional regulation** capacities vary among participants
- **Trauma** can dysregulate the nervous system, making participants more vulnerable
- **Catharsis** without cognitive processing may not be healing
- **Grounding techniques** help regulate overwhelming emotion

Legal Framework:

- Duty of care requires protection from emotional harm

- Informed consent includes awareness of potential emotional intensity
- Liability concerns require adequate training and support

Restorative Cycles Parallel: Emotional intensity is like the inflammatory phase of wound healing—uncomfortable but essential for healing. However, like chronic inflammation, unmanaged intensity can become destructive.

Preventive Strategies:

- Create safe space through ground rules and preparation
- Assess emotional readiness in preparation
- Provide grounding techniques training
- Ensure support persons are available
- Plan for breaks and pacing

Intervention Strategies:

- Pause and allow silence
- Validate emotions without judgment
- Offer grounding techniques (breathing, sensory awareness)
- Take breaks when needed
- Check in privately with overwhelmed participants
- Consider continuing another day if necessary

---

6. Challenge 4: Power Imbalances

Theological Foundation: The Magnificat celebrates God's reversal of human power structures—bringing down rulers, lifting up the humble. The upside-down kingdom requires that the powerful not dominate and the powerless not be silenced.

Psychological Dimensions:

- **Social power** affects who speaks, who interrupts, who influences
- **Voice** is essential for procedural justice
- **Empowerment** requires awareness, skills, opportunity, and support
- **Stereotype threat** can inhibit marginalized participants

Legal Framework:

- Equality before the law requires fair treatment
- Non-discrimination principles protect marginalized groups
- Due process requires meaningful opportunity to participate

Restorative Cycles Parallel: Power imbalances are like disruptions of homeostasis—they require regulatory mechanisms (facilitator interventions, structured processes) to restore balance.

Preventive Strategies:

- Use talking piece to equalize speaking opportunity
- Establish clear turn-taking protocols
- Provide preparation and support for marginalized participants
- Address power differences explicitly in preparation

- Consider separate meetings if power imbalance is severe

Intervention Strategies:

- Intervene when dominant voices monopolize
- Invite quieter participants to share
- Limit speaking time if necessary
- Name power dynamics openly when appropriate
- Use private conversations to address patterns

---

7. Challenge 5: Logistical Issues

Theological Foundation: The incarnation affirms that material reality matters. God became flesh, entering physical reality. Logistical details—time, place, accessibility—are not beneath theological concern.

Psychological Dimensions:

- **Physical environment** affects mood, attention, and engagement
- **Time of day** affects energy and capacity
- **Familiarity** with space affects comfort
- **Duration** affects ability to sustain engagement

Legal Framework:

- Accessibility requirements under disability laws
- Reasonable accommodation requirements
- Language access requirements

Restorative Cycles Parallel: Logistical resources are like nutrients, oxygen, and energy for healing—without them, healing cannot occur. The body requires adequate resources to regenerate.

Preventive Strategies:

- Flexible scheduling with multiple options
- Accessible venues (physical accessibility, location, comfort)
- Resource mobilization (grants, partnerships, volunteers)
- Technology options (virtual or hybrid)
- Thorough planning and contingency plans

Intervention Strategies:

- Problem-solve with participants
- Offer alternatives when planned logistics fail
- Use technology creatively
- Seek additional resources as needed
- Document challenges for future planning

Challenge Identification Checklist

Purpose: To assess which challenges are most relevant to your context and to track challenges as they arise.

Instructions: For each circle you facilitate or observe, check all challenges that apply. Add notes about specific manifestations.

Challenge	Check if Present	Specific Manifestation (What did it look like?)
☐ **Resistance**	☐	
☐ **Cultural Barriers**	☐	
☐ **Emotional Intensity**	☐	
☐ **Power Imbalances**	☐	
☐ **Logistical Issues**	☐	

Additional Challenges Not Listed:

Solution Planning Template

Purpose: To develop comprehensive strategies for each challenge, including both prevention and intervention.

Instructions: For each challenge, complete the template with specific strategies you will use.

CHALLENGE 1: RESISTANCE

Preventive Strategies (before the circle):

1. ______
2. ______
3. ______
4. ______

Intervention Strategies (during the circle):

1. ______
2. ______
3. ______
4. ______

What to avoid (counterproductive responses):

______

______

How to know if intervention is working:

When to consider postponing or ending the circle:

CHALLENGE 2: CULTURAL BARRIERS

Preventive Strategies (before the circle):

1. ___
2. ___
3. ___
4. ___

Intervention Strategies (during the circle):

1. ___
2. ___
3. ___
4. ___

Cultural resources to have available (interpreters, elders, translated materials):

How to learn from cultural mistakes:

CHALLENGE 3: EMOTIONAL INTENSITY

Preventive Strategies (before the circle):

1.
2.
3.
4.

Intervention Strategies (during the circle):

1.
2.
3.
4.

Grounding techniques to teach participants:

Support resources to have available:

Signs that emotional intensity is becoming harmful (not just uncomfortable):

CHALLENGE 4: POWER IMBALANCES

Preventive Strategies (before the circle):

1.
2.
3.
4.

Intervention Strategies (during the circle):

1.
2.
3.
4.

How to empower marginalized participants:

How to manage dominant participants:

When to meet separately with participants:

CHALLENGE 5: LOGISTICAL ISSUES

Preventive Strategies (before the circle):

1.
2.
3.
4.

Intervention Strategies (during the circle):

1. ______________________________
2. ______________________________
3. ______________________________
4. ______________________________

Contingency plans for common problems:

Problem	Backup Plan
Participant can't attend	
Venue becomes unavailable	
Technology fails	
Circle runs longer than expected	
Interpreter doesn't show	

Resources to have on hand:

____

____

____

Reflection Questions

1. Which of the five challenges do you find most intimidating as a potential facilitator? Why?

2. Which challenge have you experienced in your own life (as participant, observer, or in other contexts)? What happened? How was it handled?

3. The chapter describes challenges as "refining fire.' How might this perspective change how you respond when difficulties arise?

4. Think of a time when you witnessed someone in a position of power dominating a conversation. What could a facilitator have done to create more balance?

5. Think of a time when you witnessed someone become emotionally overwhelmed. What was helpful? What was unhelpful?

6. What cultural backgrounds are present in your community? What do you need to learn to facilitate effectively across these cultures?

7. The chapter emphasizes that resistance is not merely an obstacle but an expression of human freedom. How does this affect how you might respond to a resistant participant?

8. What logistical challenges are most common in your context? What can you do now to prepare for them?

Exercise 1: Role-Play – Addressing Resistance

Purpose: To practice responding to resistant participants.

Time: 20-30 minutes per scenario

Format: Small groups of 3-4. One person plays the resistant participant, one plays the facilitator, others observe and debrief.

Scenario A: The Reluctant Offender

Role: Offender (Marcus)

You've been ordered by the court to participate in this restorative justice circle. You don't want to be here. You think you've already paid your debt through your sentence. You're not interested in hearing from the victim. You sit with arms crossed, avoid eye contact, and give one-word answers. When the facilitator tries to engage you, you say things like:

- "I'm only here because I have to be."
- "This is a waste of my time."
- "I already said I was sorry. What more do they want?"
- "You don't understand my situation."

Role: Facilitator

Your task is to:

- Acknowledge Marcus's reluctance without judgment
- Re-emphasize voluntary nature (even with court involvement)
- Explore what might make participation meaningful for him
- Maintain connection without forcing engagement
- Decide whether to proceed or recommend postponement

Debrief Questions:

- How did the facilitator's approach affect Marcus?
- What worked? What didn't?
- How do you balance "voluntariness" with court-ordered participation?
- When would you decide to postpone?

Scenario B: The Skeptical Victim

Role: Victim (Elena)

You've been hurt badly and you're skeptical that any process can help. You agreed to this circle because your advocate suggested it, but you're not sure why you're here. You're afraid of being re-traumatized, afraid the offender won't take it seriously, afraid you'll get emotional and regret it. You say things like:

- "I don't see how this helps me."
- "He probably doesn't even care."
- "I've been through enough already."
- "What if I can't handle it?"

Role: Facilitator

Your task is to:

- Validate Elena's fears without dismissing them
- Give her control over the process
- Explain how the circle can be structured for her safety
- Ensure she knows she can withdraw at any time
- Help her identify what she might need to feel ready

Debrief Questions:

- How did the facilitator balance encouragement with respect for Elena's autonomy?
- What specific assurances were most helpful?
- How do you know when someone is "ready" versus when they need more time?

Exercise 2: Cultural Barrier Scenarios

Purpose: To practice navigating cultural differences in restorative circles.

Instructions: For each scenario, discuss:

- What cultural dynamics might be at play?
- What should the facilitator do?

Scenario 1: Direct vs. Indirect Communication

A facilitator from a culture that values direct, explicit communication is facilitating a circle with participants from a culture that values indirect, implicit communication. The facilitator keeps asking direct questions: "What do you want from the offender?" "How did that make you feel?" The participants seem uncomfortable and give short, vague answers.

What's happening?

What should the facilitator do?

Scenario 2: The Role of Elders

In a circle involving Indigenous participants, an elder is present. The facilitator, not from this culture, keeps trying to facilitate "equally" by giving everyone equal time. But in this culture, the elder's voice carries special weight and should be heard first and with deference. Participants are becoming uncomfortable.

What's happening?

What should the facilitator do?

Scenario 3: Emotional Expression Norms

A participant from a culture that values emotional restraint is in a circle with participants from a culture that values emotional expressiveness. The expressive participants are crying, raising their voices, showing strong feelings. The restrained participant appears judgmental and withdrawn. The expressive participants feel the restrained participant doesn't care.

What's happening?

What should the facilitator do?

Scenario 4: Language Barriers

A participant has limited proficiency in the language being used in the circle. An interpreter is present, but the participant seems frustrated. They keep trying to speak directly, then stop, then look down. The interpreter is struggling to keep up with the emotional intensity.

What's happening?

What should the facilitator do?

Exercise 3: Emotional Intensity Planning

Purpose: To develop a personal plan for managing emotional intensity.

Instructions: Complete this worksheet to prepare for moments of high emotion.

Part A: Grounding Techniques

List three grounding techniques you can offer participants:

1. ______________________________
2. ______________________________
3. ______________________________

Practice one technique now. Describe your experience:

____

____

Part B: Your Own Emotional Responses

What types of emotional expression are most challenging for you?

- ☐ Anger
- ☐ Tears/grief
- ☐ Shame
- ☐ Fear
- ☐ Silence
- ☐ Other: ______________

Why do you think these are challenging?

____

What self-talk can help you stay present when these arise?

____

Part C: When to Intervene

What signs indicate that emotional intensity is becoming harmful (not just uncomfortable)?

What is your plan if this happens?

- First, I will: ______________________________
- If that doesn't work: ______________________________
- If I need to pause the circle: ______________________________
- If someone needs additional support: ______________________________

Part D: After the Circle

How will you care for yourself after facilitating an emotionally intense circle?

Who can you debrief with?

Exercise 4: Power Imbalance Case Study

Scenario:

A restorative circle involves a manager (David) and an employee (Sarah) who reported to him. Sarah filed a complaint about David's behavior—he had been dismissive, taken credit for her work, and made comments that felt demeaning. David is defensive and insists he was just "giving feedback." The circle also includes an HR representative and a facilitator.

During the circle:

- David speaks at length, using professional jargon and positioning himself as the expert.
- Sarah speaks quietly, looks down, and takes long pauses.
- When Sarah speaks, David interrupts to "clarify" or "correct."
- The HR representative defers to David, who is a long-time employee.

Questions:

1. What power imbalances are present in this scenario?

2. What should the facilitator have done in preparation to address these imbalances?

3. What should the facilitator do now, during the circle?

4. What could the facilitator say to David when he interrupts?

5. What could the facilitator say or do to support Sarah?

6. Should the facilitator meet separately with participants? When and why?

7. What agreements might help prevent future power imbalances?

Exercise 5: Logistical Planning

Purpose: To practice anticipating and addressing logistical challenges.

Instructions: For each category, list potential challenges and solutions.

Category	Potential Challenges	Solutions/Contingencies
Scheduling		
Venue/Accessibility		
Technology		
Materials		
Participant Needs (childcare, transportation, etc.)		
Safety/Security		

Category	Potential Challenges	Solutions/Contingencies
Unexpected Events		

Create a Logistics Checklist for Your Context:

- ☐ ____
- ☐ ____
- ☐ ____
- ☐ ____
- ☐ ____
- ☐ ____

Circle Practice: "A Challenge I've Faced"

Purpose: To share experiences of challenges and how they were navigated, building collective wisdom.

Time: 45–60 minutes

Materials: Talking piece, comfortable seating

Opening (5 minutes):

- Welcome participants.
- Remind of confidentiality.
- Introduce the prompt: "Share a challenge you have faced in your life—not necessarily related to restorative justice. It could be a personal struggle, a conflict, a difficult situation. How did you navigate it? What helped? What did you learn?"

Check-In Round (10 minutes):

- Pass the talking piece. Each person shares their name and one word about how they're arriving.

Sharing Round (20–30 minutes):

- Pass the talking piece. Each person who wishes responds to the prompt.
- Allow silence between speakers.
- No cross-talk or response.

Reflection Round (10 minutes):

- Pass the talking piece. Each person shares: "What did I learn from hearing about others' challenges and how they navigated them?"

Closing (5 minutes):

- Thank participants.
- Note the wisdom and resilience in the room.
- Close with a moment of silence.

Practical Assignment: Challenge Observation and Analysis

Purpose: To apply chapter learning to real situations.

Instructions:

1. **Observe** a restorative circle, meeting, or group process where challenges might arise. If none is available, observe a workplace meeting, community gathering, or family discussion.
2. **Identify** any challenges that emerged (resistance, power imbalances, emotional intensity, cultural barriers, logistical issues).
3. **Analyze** using this framework:

Question	Your Response
What challenge(s) did you observe?	
How did they manifest? (Specific behaviors, dynamics)	
How were they addressed (or not)?	

Question	Your Response
What preventive strategies could have helped?	
What intervention strategies might have worked?	
What did you learn from this observation?	

4. **Write a 1-2 page reflection** on what you observed and what you learned about navigating challenges.

Facilitator Notes for Chapter 8

Before the Session:

1. **Read Chapter 8 thoroughly.** The challenges chapter is essential preparation for real-world practice. Familiarize yourself with all five challenges and the theological, psychological, and practical dimensions of each.
2. **Prepare for emotional depth.** Participants may share personal experiences of challenges. Create a safe container.
3. **Gather materials:**
    - Challenge Identification Checklist copies

- Solution Planning templates
- Role-play scenarios printed
- Grounding technique resources

Session Outline (3–3.5 hours):

Segment	Time	Activity
Opening	10 min	Welcome, check-in, review objectives
Key Concepts	25 min	Present five challenges and frameworks
Challenge Identification	10 min	Individual reflection on most intimidating challenge
Solution Planning	20 min	Individual work on planning templates
Role-Play: Resistance	25 min	Practice with resistant participant scenarios
Break	10 min	

Segment	Time	Activity
Cultural Barrier Scenarios	20 min	Small group discussion
Emotional Intensity Planning	15 min	Individual worksheet
Power Imbalance Case Study	20 min	Small group analysis
Logistical Planning	15 min	Group brainstorm
Circle Practice	20 min	"A Challenge I've Faced"
Closing & Assignment	5 min	Review observation assignment

Key Teaching Points:

1. **Challenges are normal.** They are not signs of failure but part of the process. Expect them; prepare for them.
2. **Prevention is better than intervention.** Most challenges can be minimized through thorough preparation.

3. **Principles apply to challenges too.** How you address a challenge should itself be restorative—respectful, inclusive, accountable.
4. **Know your limits.** Some challenges require pausing the circle, seeking help, or referring elsewhere. Wisdom includes knowing when not to proceed.
5. **Learn from every challenge.** Each difficulty is an opportunity to grow as a facilitator.

Common Questions:

- **Q: "What if multiple challenges occur at once?"** A: Prioritize safety first. Then address the challenge most disrupting the process. You may need to pause and consult.
- **Q: "How do I know if emotional intensity is healing or harmful?"** A: Signs of harm: participant dissociates, cannot regain regulation, expresses feeling worse, wants to leave but can't. Trust your instincts; check in.
- **Q: "What if a participant's resistance is justified?"** A: Listen. They may have valid concerns about the process. Resistance can be information about what needs to change.
- **Q: "How do I handle power imbalances when the powerful person is my supervisor or funder?"** A: This is challenging. Be clear about your role as facilitator. If you cannot be impartial, you should not facilitate. Consider co-facilitation with someone who can balance.
- **Q: "What if I make a mistake in handling a challenge?"** A: Acknowledge it, apologize, and try to repair. Your own accountability models restorative values.

After the Session:

- Follow up on observation assignment.
- Collect solution planning templates if desired.
- Prepare for Chapter 9 on psychological and emotional impact.

Personal Journal: Chapter 8

Date: ______________

The challenge I most need to prepare for:

A preventive strategy I will implement:

An intervention strategy I want to practice:

What I learned about myself from this chapter:

A question I'm still holding:

Key Terms Glossary for Chapter 8

Term	Definition
Resistance	Reluctance to participate; denial of responsibility; skepticism
Cultural Barriers	Differences in communication, values, and expectations across cultures

Term	Definition
Emotional Intensity	Overwhelming emotions that can disrupt circle process
Power Imbalance	Unequal status, authority, or resources affecting participation
Logistical Issues	Practical challenges of time, place, accessibility, resources
Reactance	Motivational state aroused when freedom is threatened; can intensify resistance
Cognitive Distortions	Biased thinking patterns that support denial or minimization
Grounding Techniques	Practices that help regulate overwhelming emotion
Procedural Justice	Fairness of the process (voice, neutrality, respect, trust)

Term	Definition
Allostatic Load	Cumulative wear and tear of chronic stress
Window of Tolerance	Range of arousal within which individuals can function effectively
Titration	Gradual, controlled exposure to challenging material

---

"*The challenges that arise in restorative justice circles are not evidence of failure but evidence of fidelity. They are the growing pains of communities learning to address harm differently, the birth pangs of new relationships struggling to be born, the refining fire that tests and strengthens restorative practice.*" — Dr. Maxwell Shimba

CHAPTER 09

The Psychological and Emotional Impact of Restorative Justice

Learning Objectives

By completing this chapter, you will be able to:

- **Identify the psychological and emotional benefits** of restorative justice for victims, offenders, and communities
- **Recognize the potential risks** of restorative processes, including re-traumatization

- **Develop emotional awareness** of the experiences of all circle participants
- **Apply trauma-informed principles** to restorative practice
- **Create strategies** to maximize benefits and minimize harm
- **Understand the facilitator's role** in supporting emotional safety and healing

Key Concepts from Chapter 9

1. The Healing of the Soul

The psychological and emotional dimensions of restorative justice are not secondary effects or incidental benefits. They are at the very heart of what restorative justice seeks to accomplish—the healing of wounds that are not merely legal or material but deeply personal, relational, and spiritual. Crime and conflict wound souls, shatter trust, and disrupt inner peace. Restorative justice circles become spaces where these wounds can be acknowledged, tended, and healed.

2. The Biblical Foundation of Emotional Healing

Biblical Concept	Application to Restorative Justice
Lament (Psalms)	Giving voice to suffering, anger, and protest
Shalom	Comprehensive well-being through right relationship

Biblical Concept	Application to Restorative Justice
Heart of flesh (Ezekiel 36:26)	Transformation from hardness to compassion
Comfort (2 Corinthians 1:4)	Receiving and extending God's comfort
Bearing burdens (Galatians 6:2)	Carrying each other's emotional loads

3. Psychological and Emotional Benefits

For Whom	Benefits
Victims	Healing and closure; validation; restored voice; reduced fear and anger; post-traumatic growth; enhanced self-esteem and empowerment
Offenders	Empathy development; reintegrative shame; reduced recidivism; restored moral agency; hope and self-efficacy

For Whom	Benefits
Com-muni-ties	Strengthened bonds; collective efficacy; restored trust; social capital; community resilience

4. Empathy: The Expansion of the Heart

Empathy—the capacity to understand and share the feelings of another—is one of the most significant psychological benefits of restorative justice.

Theological Foundation: The prophet Ezekiel promises God will "remove from you your heart of stone and give you a heart of flesh" (Ezekiel 36:26). The heart of stone cannot feel another's pain; the heart of flesh can be touched, can feel with and for others.

Psychological Research:

- **Neural basis:** Mirror neurons enable us to "mirror" others' experiences
- **Perspective-taking:** Imagining another's experience increases empathy
- **Contact theory:** Structured contact under appropriate conditions reduces prejudice and increases empathy

Restorative Cycles Parallel: Empathy development is like neural plasticity—the formation of new neural connections that literally rewire the brain for greater compassion.

5. Reduced Recidivism: The Transformation of the Offender

One of the most consistently documented benefits of restorative justice is its effect on recidivism—the likelihood that offenders will reoffend.

Theological Foundation: *Metanoia* (repentance) is a change of mind that issues in changed behavior. John the Baptist demands "fruit in keeping with repentance" (Luke 3:8). Zacchaeus's fourfold restitution is repentance with fruit.

Psychological Research:

- **Cognitive transformation:** Changes in identity, values, and worldviews
- **Social bonds:** Strengthened connections to prosocial networks
- **Procedural justice:** Fair treatment enhances legitimacy and compliance
- **Reintegrative shame:** Shame focused on behavior, not person, reduces reoffending

Restorative Cycles Parallel: Recidivism reduction is like synaptic pruning—eliminating unused or harmful neural connections and developing new, more adaptive patterns.

6. Healing and Closure: The Restoration of the Victim

For victims, restorative justice offers opportunities for healing and closure that conventional justice rarely provides.

Theological Foundation: The Psalms of lament give voice to suffering. Jesus restores voice to the voiceless—the mute man, the hemorrhaging woman, the blind beggar.

Psychological Research:

- **Narrative integration:** Telling one's story in a safe setting enables integration of traumatic memories
- **Post-traumatic growth:** Positive psychological changes can result from struggling with trauma
- **Closure:** Knowing that the offender has been held accountable, receiving acknowledgment and apology

Restorative Cycles Parallel: Victim healing is like scar formation—not identical to original tissue but strong, functional, and integrated into ongoing life.

7. Enhanced Self-Esteem and Empowerment: The Restoration of Agency

Victimization is fundamentally disempowering. Restorative justice restores victims' agency by giving them voice and involving them in determining reparation.

Theological Foundation: The *imago Dei*—every person bears God's image and possesses intrinsic dignity. This dignity cannot be taken away by victimization.

Psychological Research:

- **Empowerment:** Increasing capacity to make choices and influence outcomes
- **Self-efficacy:** Belief that one can successfully execute actions to produce desired outcomes
- **Locus of control:** Shifting from external to internal through successful action

Restorative Cycles Parallel: Empowerment is like active immunity—stronger and more durable than passive receipt of services.

8. Strengthened Community Bonds: The Restoration of Relationship

Restorative justice strengthens the bonds that constitute community.

Theological Foundation: The body of Christ (1 Corinthians 12)—if one part suffers, all suffer; if one is honored, all rejoice. *Koinonia*—fellowship, sharing, participation.

Psychological Research:

- **Social capital:** Networks of relationships, norms of reciprocity, and trust
- **Collective efficacy:** Shared belief that community can work together to achieve common goals
- **Community resilience:** Capacity to withstand and recover from adversity

Restorative Cycles Parallel: Community strengthening is like ecological succession—development toward greater complexity, diversity, and stability.

SECTION II: POTENTIAL RISKS AND CHALLENGES

9. Re-Traumatization: The Wound Reopened

The emotional intensity of restorative circles, while potentially healing, also carries risks. For participants with trauma histories, the process can trigger traumatic responses.

Theological Foundation: The "wounded healer"—one whose own wounds become the source of healing for others. Jesus' wounds are central even after resurrection.

Psychological Research:

- **Trauma:** Overwhelming of coping capacity; memories stored fragmented
- **Triggers:** Stimuli that evoke traumatic responses
- **Retraumatization:** Recurrence of traumatic symptoms
- **Trauma-informed practice:** Safety, trustworthiness, choice, collaboration, empowerment

Restorative Cycles Parallel: Retraumatization risk is like chronic inflammation—acute inflammation that does not resolve becomes destructive.

10. Resistance and Denial: The Hardened Heart

Resistance and denial from offenders can undermine restorative processes and harm participants.

Theological Foundation: Pharaoh's hardened heart—refusal to acknowledge reality. Yet hearts can soften—the prodigal son "came to his senses."

Psychological Research:

- **Denial:** Refusal to acknowledge reality
- **Minimization:** Downplaying harm
- **Cognitive distortions:** Biased thinking supporting offending

- **Motivational interviewing:** Expressing empathy, developing discrepancy, rolling with resistance, supporting self-efficacy

Restorative Cycles Parallel: Resistance is like scar tissue adhesions—healing gone awry, creating new problems.

11. Power Imbalances: The Unequal Yoke

Power imbalances among participants can undermine fairness and effectiveness.

Theological Foundation: The Magnificat—God brings down rulers, lifts up the humble. The upside-down kingdom requires that the powerful not dominate.

Psychological Research:

- **Social power:** High-power individuals speak more, interrupt more, influence more
- **Voice:** Essential for procedural justice
- **Procedural justice:** Voice, neutrality, respect, trustworthiness

Restorative Cycles Parallel: Power imbalances are like homeostasis disruption—requiring regulatory mechanisms to restore balance.

12. Emotional Burnout: The Exhaustion of Compassion

Facilitators and participants may experience emotional burnout from sustained engagement with intense emotions.

Theological Foundation: Elijah under the broom tree—"I have had enough, Lord." God's response: rest, nourishment, companionship, renewed mission.

Psychological Research:

- **Compassion fatigue:** Emotional exhaustion from caring for suffering others
- **Vicarious trauma:** Transformation of helpers' inner experience
- **Burnout:** Emotional exhaustion, depersonalization, reduced accomplishment
- **Self-care:** Physical, emotional, social, spiritual, professional

Restorative Cycles Parallel: Burnout is like allostatic load—cumulative wear and tear of chronic stress without adequate recovery.

Emotional Awareness Exercise

Purpose: To develop awareness of the emotional experiences of all circle participants, enabling more empathetic and effective facilitation.

Instructions: For each role, list the emotions they might experience before, during, and after a restorative circle. Consider both positive and negative emotions.

EMOTIONS EXPERIENCED BY VICTIMS

Before the Circle:

Emotion	What might trigger this?

During the Circle:

Emotion	What might trigger this?

After the Circle:

Emotion	What might trigger this?

EMOTIONS EXPERIENCED BY OFFENDERS

Before the Circle:

Emotion	What might trigger this?

During the Circle:

Emotion	What might trigger this?

After the Circle:

Emotion	What might trigger this?

EMOTIONS EXPERIENCED BY FACILITATORS

Before the Circle:

Emotion	What might trigger this?

During the Circle:

Emotion	What might trigger this?

After the Circle:

Emotion	What might trigger this?

EMOTIONS EXPERIENCED BY COMMUNITY MEMBERS

Before the Circle:

Emotion	What might trigger this?

During the Circle:

Emotion	What might trigger this?

After the Circle:

Emotion	What might trigger this?

Reflection Questions on Emotional Awareness:

1. Which emotions did you find easiest to identify? Which were hardest?

2. Were you surprised by any emotions you listed?

3. How might understanding these emotional experiences help you as a facilitator?

4. Which participant's emotional experience do you find most challenging to imagine? Why?

5. How can you prepare to support each of these emotional experiences?

Trauma-Informed Checklist

Purpose: To ensure restorative circles are conducted in ways that recognize and respond to trauma, minimizing the risk of re-traumatization.

Instructions: Before each circle, review this checklist. During and after the circle, note how well each principle was upheld.

PRINCIPLE 1: SAFETY

Question	Yes	Partially	No	Notes
Is the physical space safe and accessible?	☐	☐	☐	

Question	Yes	Par-tially	No	Notes
Is the emotional environment supportive?	☐	☐	☐	
Have ground rules been established to prevent harm?	☐	☐	☐	
Are emergency procedures in place?	☐	☐	☐	
Do participants know they can request breaks?	☐	☐	☐	
Are support persons available if needed?	☐	☐	☐	

Safety Action Items:

____

____

____

PRINCIPLE 2: TRUSTWORTHINESS

Question	Yes	Partially	No	Notes
Have I been transparent about the process?	☐	☐	☐	
Have I been consistent in my communication?	☐	☐	☐	
Have I followed through on commitments?	☐	☐	☐	
Have I been clear about confidentiality and its limits?	☐	☐	☐	
Do participants know what to expect?	☐	☐	☐	

Trustworthiness Action Items:

PRINCIPLE 3: CHOICE

Question	Yes	Partially	No	Notes
Have participants been informed of their right to withdraw?	☐	☐	☐	
Do participants have choices about their level of participation?	☐	☐	☐	
Can participants choose to pass during sharing?	☐	☐	☐	
Are there options for breaks, support persons, or accommodations?	☐	☐	☐	
Is consent ongoing, not just initial?	☐	☐	☐	

Choice Action Items:

PRINCIPLE 4: COLLABORATION

Question	Yes	Partially	No	Notes
Are participants treated as partners, not problems?	☐	☐	☐	
Is decision-making shared, not imposed?	☐	☐	☐	
Do participants have meaningful input into agreements?	☐	☐	☐	
Is power sharing evident in the process?	☐	☐	☐	

Question	Yes	Par-tially	No	Notes
Are diverse perspectives valued and included?	☐	☐	☐	

Collaboration Action Items:

PRINCIPLE 5: EMPOWERMENT

Question	Yes	Par-tially	No	Notes
Are participants' strengths recognized and built upon?	☐	☐	☐	
Do participants leave with a greater sense of agency?	☐	☐	☐	

Question	Yes	Partially	No	Notes
Are voices that have been silenced being heard?	☐	☐	☐	
Is the process focused on participants' own healing?	☐	☐	☐	
Are participants connected to additional resources if needed?	☐	☐	☐	

Empowerment Action Items:

PRINCIPLE 6: CULTURAL CONSIDERATIONS

Question	Yes	Partially	No	Notes
Have I learned about participants' cultural backgrounds?	☐	☐	☐	
Are cultural practices honored appropriately?	☐	☐	☐	
Are interpreters or translated materials available if needed?	☐	☐	☐	
Have I avoided imposing my own cultural assumptions?	☐	☐	☐	
Is the process accessible across cultural differences?	☐	☐	☐	

Cultural Considerations Action Items:

Trauma-Informed Practice Self-Assessment

Purpose: To assess your own readiness to facilitate in trauma-informed ways.

Competency	I do this consistently	I do this sometimes	I need to develop this
I recognize signs of trauma (hyperarousal, avoidance, intrusion)	☐	☐	☐
I create physically and emotionally safe environments	☐	☐	☐
I maximize participants' choice and control	☐	☐	☐

Competency	I do this consistently	I do this sometimes	I need to develop this
I am transparent about processes and expectations	☐	☐	☐
I build trust through consistency and reliability	☐	☐	☐
I focus on strengths and support self-advocacy	☐	☐	☐
I collaborate with participants rather than doing things to them	☐	☐	☐
I adapt practices to cultural contexts	☐	☐	☐

Competency	I do this consistently	I do this sometimes	I need to develop this
I connect participants with trauma treatment resources	☐	☐	☐
I use grounding techniques when participants are overwhelmed	☐	☐	☐
I pace the process to stay within participants' window of tolerance	☐	☐	☐
I practice self-care to prevent vicarious trauma	☐	☐	☐

My top three priorities for trauma-informed growth:

1. ______________________________
2. ______________________________
3. ______________________________

Reflection Questions

1. The chapter describes restorative justice as addressing "the healing of the soul." What does this mean to you? How does it affect how you understand the purpose of circles?

2. Think of a time when you experienced empathy—either giving or receiving it. What made that experience powerful? How can restorative circles create conditions for empathy?

3. The chapter distinguishes between "stigmatizing shame" (I am a bad person) and "reintegrative shame" (I did a bad thing). Why is this distinction important for offender transformation?

4. Have you ever experienced the "injustice gap"—a discrepancy between what you needed and what you received after being harmed? What would have narrowed that gap?

5. The chapter describes victims' healing as "scar formation"—not identical to original tissue but strong and functional. How might this metaphor help victims have realistic expectations?

6. What is your own emotional regulation capacity? How do you typically respond when others are experiencing intense emotions? What do you need to work on?

7. The "wounded healer" concept suggests that our own wounds can become sources of healing for others. How might your own experiences of wounding and healing equip you for restorative work? What cautions does this require?

8. How will you practice self-care to prevent burnout and vicarious trauma?

Exercise 1: Empathy Development Practice

Purpose: To practice the cognitive and emotional skills that build empathy.

Instructions: For each scenario, write:

- What the person might be feeling
- What they might need
- What you could say or do to show empathy

Scenario 1: A Victim's Testimony

A victim is describing the impact of a burglary: "I can't sleep anymore. Every noise wakes me up. I keep thinking they're coming back. I know it's irrational, but I can't stop it. My home doesn't feel like home anymore."

What might they be feeling?

What might they need?

What could you say or do to show empathy?

Scenario 2: An Offender's Remorse

An offender says: "I never thought about how she would feel. I was just thinking about myself, about what I needed. Hearing her talk... I feel sick. I can't believe I did that to someone."

What might they be feeling?

What might they need?

What could you say or do to show empathy?

Scenario 3: A Community Member's Fear

A neighbor says: "Since the vandalism, I don't let my kids play outside like I used to. I used to know everyone on this block. Now I don't trust anyone. This used to be a good neighborhood."

What might they be feeling?

What might they need?

What could you say or do to show empathy?

Scenario 4: A Facilitator's Exhaustion

A fellow facilitator shares: "I've done three circles this week with really heavy cases. I can't stop thinking about them. I had trouble sleeping last night. I'm not sure how much longer I can keep doing this."

What might they be feeling?

What might they need?

What could you say or do to show empathy?

Exercise 2: Grounding Techniques Practice

Purpose: To practice grounding techniques that can be offered to overwhelmed participants.

Instructions: Practice each technique yourself. Then reflect on how you might offer it to others.

Technique 1: Breath Awareness

Instructions: "Take a slow breath in through your nose... and out through your mouth. Notice the air moving in and out. If your mind wanders, just bring it back to your breath. Let's do that together a few times."

Your experience:

When might you offer this?

Technique 2: 5-4-3-2-1 Sensory Grounding

Instructions: "Name 5 things you can see... 4 things you can feel (your feet on the floor, your hands on your legs)... 3 things you can hear... 2 things you can smell... 1 thing you can taste."

Your experience:

When might you offer this?

Technique 3: Physical Grounding

Instructions: "Press your feet firmly into the floor. Feel the ground supporting you. Press your hands together. Notice the sensation. You are here, in this room, safe."

Your experience:

When might you offer this?

Technique 4: Safe Place Visualization

Instructions: "Close your eyes and imagine a place where you feel completely safe. It can be real or imagined. Notice what you see, hear, smell, feel there. You can return to this place anytime you need to."

Your experience:

When might you offer this?

Exercise 3: Window of Tolerance Mapping

Purpose: To understand the concept of "window of tolerance" and how it applies to circle participants.

The Concept: The window of tolerance is the range of arousal within which a person can function effectively. Above this window is hyperarousal (overwhelmed, reactive, unable to process). Below is hypoarousal (shut down, dissociated, unable to engage). Trauma-informed practice keeps participants within their windows.

Instructions: For each scenario, identify:

- Is the person in their window, hyperaroused, or hypoaroused?
- What could help them return to their window?

Scenario A: A victim is speaking rapidly, voice shaking, tears flowing. They keep repeating the same details and seem unable to hear the facilitator's gentle prompts.

Window status: ☐ In window ☐ Hyperaroused ☐ Hypoaroused

What might help?

Scenario B: An offender has gone completely silent. They are staring at the floor, not responding when spoken to, not seeming to hear what others are saying.

Window status: ☐ In window ☐ Hyperaroused ☐ Hypoaroused

What might help?

Scenario C: A community member is speaking calmly and thoughtfully, able to listen to others and respond appropriately, showing emotion but not overwhelmed.

Window status: ☐ In window ☐ Hyperaroused ☐ Hypoaroused

What might help?

Scenario D: A facilitator notices their own heart racing, thoughts spinning, difficulty concentrating on what participants are saying.

Window status: ☐ In window ☐ Hyperaroused ☐ Hypoaroused

What might help?

Exercise 4: Self-Care Planning

Purpose: To develop a personal self-care plan to prevent burnout and vicarious trauma.

Instructions: Complete each section with specific practices you will commit to.

PHYSICAL SELF-CARE

What I will do for my body (sleep, nutrition, exercise, medical care):

Practice	When	How I'll ensure I do it

EMOTIONAL SELF-CARE

How I will process emotions (journaling, therapy, supportive relationships):

Practice	When	How I'll ensure I do it

SOCIAL SELF-CARE

Relationships that nourish me (family, friends, community):

Practice	When	How I'll ensure I do it

SPIRITUAL SELF-CARE

Practices that nurture meaning, purpose, and connection:

Practice	When	How I'll ensure I do it

PROFESSIONAL SELF-CARE

Support for my work (supervision, peer consultation, boundaries, breaks):

Practice	When	How I'll ensure I do it

WARNING SIGNS

How will I know I'm heading toward burnout?

What will I do if I notice these signs?

Circle Practice: "A Time I Felt Heard"

Purpose: To experience the healing power of being truly heard and to practice creating conditions for others to feel heard.

Time: 45–60 minutes

Materials: Talking piece, comfortable seating

Opening (5 minutes):

- Welcome participants.
- Remind of confidentiality.
- Introduce the prompt: "Share a time when you felt truly heard—when someone listened to you in a way that

made you feel understood, validated, and cared for. What made that experience powerful?"

Check-In Round (10 minutes):

- Pass the talking piece. Each person shares their name and one word about how they're arriving.

Sharing Round (20–30 minutes):

- Pass the talking piece. Each person who wishes responds to the prompt.
- Allow silence between speakers.
- No cross-talk or response.

Reflection Round (10 minutes):

- Pass the talking piece. Each person shares: "What did I learn about listening and being heard from this circle?"

Closing (5 minutes):

- Thank participants.
- Affirm the gift of listening and being listened to.
- Close with a moment of silence.

Practical Assignment: Emotional Impact Observation

Purpose: To apply chapter learning by observing emotional dynamics in a real setting.

Instructions:

1. **Observe** a restorative circle, support group, therapy session, or any gathering where people share emotionally

significant experiences. (If none is available, observe a film or video that depicts emotional sharing.)

2. **Take notes** on:
    - What emotions were expressed?
    - How did others respond?
    - What seemed to help or hinder emotional safety?
    - What would a trauma-informed facilitator have noticed?
3. **Write a 2-3 page reflection** addressing:
    - What you observed about emotional dynamics
    - How the principles of trauma-informed practice were or were not present
    - What you learned about supporting emotional safety
    - How you will apply this learning to your own facilitation

Facilitator Notes for Chapter 9

Before the Session:

1. **Read Chapter 9 thoroughly.** This chapter deals with deep emotional territory. Be prepared for participants to have strong reactions.
2. **Prepare for emotional depth.** The exercises invite personal reflection. Create a safe container with clear confidentiality.
3. **Gather grounding technique resources.** Have handouts or cards with grounding exercises.
4. **Know your referral resources.** If participants need additional support, have counseling resources available.

Session Outline (3–3.5 hours):

Segment	Time	Activity
Opening	10 min	Welcome, check-in, review objectives
Key Concepts	25 min	Present benefits, risks, and trauma-informed principles
Emotional Awareness Exercise	20 min	Individual work on emotions of victims, offenders, facilitators
Trauma-Informed Checklist	15 min	Review and discuss each principle
Empathy Practice	15 min	Small group scenario work
Grounding Techniques Practice	15 min	Practice techniques in pairs
Break	10 min	

Segment	Time	Activity
Window of Tolerance	15 min	Mapping exercise
Self-Care Planning	20 min	Individual work on self-care plan
Circle Practice	25 min	"A Time I Felt Heard"
Closing & Assignment	5 min	Review observation assignment

Key Teaching Points:

1. **Emotions are not problems to be fixed.** They are information about what matters. Honor them.
2. **Trauma-informed practice is not optional.** Given the prevalence of trauma, it is essential for safe, effective facilitation.
3. **The facilitator's own emotional health matters.** You cannot pour from an empty cup. Self-care is not selfish.
4. **The window of tolerance concept is practical.** Learn to recognize when participants are in or out of their window.

5. **Healing is possible.** The research is clear: restorative justice produces significant psychological benefits. Hold hope.

Common Questions:

- **Q: "How do I know if someone has trauma?"**
  A: You may not know. Assume trauma is present and act accordingly. Trauma-informed practice benefits everyone.
- **Q: "What if I get triggered by something a participant says?"**
  A: It happens. Have a plan: grounding techniques, support from co-facilitator, debriefing afterward. Know your limits.
- **Q: "Can restorative justice retraumatize someone?"**
  A: Yes, if not done carefully. That's why trauma-informed practice is essential.
- **Q: "How do I balance emotional safety with allowing authentic expression?"**
  A: Create the container (ground rules, preparation, facilitator presence). Then trust the process. Intervene if safety is threatened.
- **Q: "What if a participant needs more support than I can provide?"**
  A: Have referral resources ready. Your role is facilitator, not therapist. Know your boundaries.

After the Session:

- Check in privately with anyone who seemed distressed.
- Follow up on observation assignment.
- Prepare for Chapter 10 on restorative justice in schools.

Personal Journal: Chapter 9

Date: ______________

The most important thing I learned about emotional impact:

An emotion I need to be more aware of in myself:

A grounding technique I will practice:

How I will practice trauma-informed facilitation:

One thing I will do for my own self-care:

A question I'm still holding:

Key Terms Glossary for Chapter 9

Term	Definition
Empathy	Capacity to understand and share others' feelings
Reintegrative Shame	Shame focused on behavior, with respect for person

Term	Definition
Stigmatizing Shame	Shame focused on person as bad, leading to exclusion
Post-Traumatic Growth	Positive psychological change after trauma
Closure	Sense of completion enabling moving forward
Injustice Gap	Discrepancy between desired and actual resolution
Compassion Fatigue	Emotional exhaustion from caring for suffering others
Vicarious Trauma	Transformation of helpers' inner experience through empathic engagement
Burnout	Emotional exhaustion, depersonalization, reduced accomplishment

Term	Definition
Window of Tolerance	Range of arousal within which individuals can function effectively
Grounding Techniques	Practices that help regulate overwhelming emotion
Trauma-Informed Practice	Approach recognizing trauma's prevalence and effects; prioritizing safety, choice, trust, collaboration, empowerment
Allostatic Load	Cumulative wear and tear of chronic stress

"The psychological and emotional dimensions of restorative justice are not secondary effects or incidental benefits. They are at the very heart of what restorative justice seeks to accomplish—the healing of wounds that are not merely legal or material but deeply personal, relational, and spiritual." — Dr. Maxwell Shimba

CHAPTER 10

Restorative Justice Circles in Schools

Learning Objectives

By completing this chapter, you will be able to:

- **Understand the unique role** of restorative justice in educational settings
- **Identify the multiple purposes** of circles in schools (conflict resolution, behavior improvement, community building, emotional support, prevention)
- **Design restorative responses** to common school challenges (bullying, classroom disruption, teacher-student conflict)
- **Develop a comprehensive school restorative policy**

- **Integrate restorative practices** into school culture and discipline systems
- **Apply trauma-informed and developmentally appropriate approaches** with students

Key Concepts from Chapter 10

1. The School as Covenantal Community

The school is more than a building where instruction occurs; it is a community where young people are formed—intellectually, socially, morally, and spiritually. Within its walls, students learn not only mathematics and literature but also how to relate to others, how to resolve conflicts, how to take responsibility for their actions, and how to contribute to the common good.

Theological Foundation: The people of Israel were formed through practices of teaching and learning—the transmission of Torah from parents to children. Jesus was called "Teacher" (*didaskalos*) more frequently than any other title. The early church understood itself as a learning community devoted to "the apostles' teaching" (Acts 2:42).

2. Why Traditional Discipline Fails

Traditional Approach	Problem
Zero-tolerance policies	Remove students from learning; exacerbate problems

Traditional Approach	Problem
Suspension/Expulsion	Increase alienation and dropout risk
Punitive responses	Do not address root causes or teach new skills
Exclusionary discipline	Disproportionately affects students of color and with disabilities

3. The Five Purposes of Restorative Circles in Schools

Purpose	Description
Conflict Resolution	Addressing disputes constructively; involving all affected parties
Behavior Improvement	Forming character through accountability and reflection, not just punishment
Community Building	Strengthening relationships and sense of belonging for all

Purpose	Description
Emotional Support	Providing safe space for students to share feelings and receive support
Prevention and Education	Teaching restorative values and skills before problems occur

4. Types of Circles in Schools

Circle Type	Purpose	Frequency
Community-Building Circles	Build relationships, check-in, share experiences	Daily/Weekly
Curriculum Circles	Explore academic content through dialogue	As needed
Problem-Solving Circles	Address specific issues affecting the class	As needed
Conflict Resolution Circles	Respond to specific incidents of harm	As needed

Circle Type	Purpose	Frequency
Re-entry Circles	Welcome students back after absence/suspension	As needed
Staff Circles	Build community among teachers and staff	Regular

5. The Restorative Pyramid in Schools

text
[Tier 3: Intensive Intervention]
(Intensive circles for serious incidents,
re-entry after suspension, ongoing support)
[Tier 2: Targeted Intervention]
(Response circles for specific conflicts,
small group circles for at-risk students)
[Tier 1: Universal Prevention]
(Daily community-building circles,
restorative language and practices
integrated into all classrooms)

6. Key Elements for School Implementation

Element	Description
Leadership Commitment	Administrators must understand and support restorative approaches
Staff Training	All staff need training in restorative philosophy and practices
Student Involvement	Students should be trained as peer facilitators and leaders
Family Engagement	Parents/guardians must understand and support restorative approaches
Policy Alignment	School discipline policies must be revised to incorporate restorative options
Ongoing Support	Coaching, mentoring, and professional development sustain implementation

School Scenario Exercise

Purpose: To practice designing restorative responses to common school challenges.

Instructions: For each scenario, complete the response template. Consider all affected parties, preparation needed, circle process, agreements, and follow-up.

SCENARIO 1: BULLYING

Background:

Maria, a 7th-grade student, has been the target of persistent bullying by a group of three classmates. The bullying includes mocking her appearance, excluding her from group activities, and spreading rumors on social media. Maria has started skipping school, her grades have dropped, and she seems withdrawn and anxious. The school has suspended the offenders twice, but the behavior continues. Maria's parents are demanding that the school "do something."

Those Affected:

Stakeholder	How Affected
Maria (victim)	
The three bullies (offenders)	
Other students who witnessed	
Maria's parents	

Stakeholder	How Affected
The bullies' parents	
Teachers/staff	
The broader school community	

Restorative Response Design:

1. Preparation Needed:

Who needs individual meetings?	What concerns might they have?	What information do they need?

2. Circle Participants:

Who should be included in the circle?

3. Opening (Ritual, Ground Rules, Purpose):

What opening ritual would be appropriate?

____

What ground rules are essential?

____

How will you state the purpose?

____

4. Sharing (What questions will guide sharing?):

For Maria: ________________________________

For the bullies: ________________________________

For other students:

____

For parents: ________________________________

5. Discussion (What needs to be explored?):

____

____

6. Agreement (Possible restorative actions):

Action	Responsible Party	Timeline

7. Follow-Up:

How and when will you check progress?

---

8. Additional Supports Needed:

What other interventions might be needed (counseling, mentoring, etc.)?

SCENARIO 2: CLASSROOM DISRUPTION

Background:

In a 10th-grade history class, a student named Jamal has been frequently disruptive—talking during instruction, mak ng sarcastic comments, refusing to participate in group work, and occasionally walking out of class. His teacher, Mr. Chen, has tried various strategies: talking with Jamal privately, calling home, giving detention, and sending him to the office. Nothing has worked. The disruption is affecting other students' learning, and Mr. Chen is feeling frustrated and ineffective. Jamal says the class is "boring" and Mr. Chen "doesn't like him."

Those Affected:

Stakeholder	How Affected
Mr. Chen (teacher)	
Jamal (student)	
Other students in class	
Jamal's parents/guardians	
School administration	

Restorative Response Design:

1. Preparation Needed:

Who needs individual meetings?	What concerns might they have?	What information do they need?

2. Circle Participants:

Who should be included in the circle?

---

3. Opening (Ritual, Ground Rules, Purpose):

What opening ritual would be appropriate?

What ground rules are essential?

How will you state the purpose?

---

4. Sharing (What questions will guide sharing?):

For Mr. Chen: ____

For Jamal: ____

For other students:

____

5. Discussion (What needs to be explored?):

Consider: What might be underlying Jamal's behavior? What does Mr. Chen need? What do other students need? What would make the classroom work for everyone?

6. Agreement (Possible restorative actions):

Action	Responsible Party	Timeline

7. Follow-Up:

How and when will you check progress?

8. Additional Supports Needed:

What other interventions might be needed (academic support, counseling, mentoring)?

SCENARIO 3: TEACHER-STUDENT CONFLICT

Background:

Ms. Rodriguez, a high school English teacher, had a heated exchange with a student, Devon, in class. Devon was on his phone; Ms. Rodriguez asked him to put it away; Devon refused; Ms. Rodriguez raised her voice; Devon responded with disrespectful language; Ms. Rodriguez sent him to the office. Since then, the relationship has deteriorated. Devon refuses to participate in her class, sits with his hood up, and doesn't do assignments. Ms. Rodriguez feels disrespected and is frustrated that Devon is falling behind. Other students are uncomfortable with the tension. Both parties are stuck.

Those Affected:

Stakeholder	How Affected
Ms. Rodriguez	
Devon	

Stakeholder	How Affected
Other students in class	
Devon's parents	
School administration	

Restorative Response Design:

1. Preparation Needed:

Who needs individual meetings?	What concerns might they have?	What information do they need?

2. Circle Participants:

Who should be included in the circle?

3. Opening (Ritual, Ground Rules, Purpose):

What opening ritual would be appropriate?

What ground rules are essential?

How will you state the purpose?

4. Sharing (What questions will guide sharing?):

For Ms. Rodriguez:
____

For Devon: ____

For other students (if included):
____

5. Discussion (What needs to be explored?):

Consider: What happened from each perspective? What was each person feeling? What did each need in that moment? What do they need now to move forward?

6. Agreement (Possible restorative actions):

Action	Responsible Party	Timeline

7. Follow-Up:

How and when will you check progress?

---

8. Additional Supports Needed:

What other interventions might be needed?

Exercise 1: Proactive Community-Building Circle Design

Purpose: To practice designing proactive circles that build community and prevent conflict.

Instructions: Design a 20-minute community-building circle for a specific classroom context.

Context: ______________________________ (grade level, subject, class size, known dynamics)

Purpose of this circle: ________________________________

Opening (2-3 minutes):

Welcoming statement:

____

Purpose statement:

____

Brief ritual or centering:

____

Ground rules to review:

____

Check-In Round (5 minutes):

Prompt: ________________________________

Sharing Round (8-10 minutes):

Prompt: ________________________________

Closing Round (3-5 minutes):

Reflection prompt: ____

Closing words:

____

Materials needed: ____

How this circle builds community: ____

____

Exercise 2: Integrating Circles into Curriculum

Purpose: To explore how restorative circles can support academic learning.

Instructions: Choose a subject and topic. Design a curriculum circle that explores academic content through dialogue.

Subject: ____

Topic: ____

Grade Level: ____

Learning Objectives:

1. ____
2. ____

3. ______

Circle Prompt (open-ended question related to content):

______

How the circle format supports learning:

______

How you will ensure all students can participate:

______

How you will connect circle discussion to further learning:

______

______

Exercise 3: Responding to Resistance from Staff

Purpose: To practice addressing common concerns from teachers and administrators about restorative justice.

Instructions: For each concern, draft a respectful, evidence-informed response.

Concern	Your Response
"This is just letting kids off easy. They need consequences."	
"I don't have time for circles. I have curriculum to cover."	
"What about the victims? This seems focused on the offenders."	
"We've tried programs before. They don't last."	
"This won't work with my toughest kids."	
"Parents will think we're being soft."	
"What about serious incidents like fights or weapons?"	

Exercise 4: Peer Facilitator Training Outline

Purpose: To design a training program for student peer facilitators.

Instructions: Outline a training program for high school students who will co-facilitate restorative circles.

Training Goals:

1. ____________________
2. ____________________
3. ____________________
4. ____________________

Module 1: Restorative Principles

Key content: ____________________

Activities: ____________________

Module 2: Facilitation Skills

Key content: ____________________

Activities: ____________________

Module 3: Circle Process

Key content: ____________________

Activities: ____________________

Module 4: Challenging Situations

Key content: ____________________

Activities: ______________________________

Module 5: Ethics and Boundaries

Key content: ______________________________

Activities: ______________________________

Practice Requirements:

Ongoing Support:

Practical Assignment: Create a School Restorative Policy Draft

Purpose: To develop a comprehensive restorative justice policy for a school.

Instructions: Using the template below, draft a restorative justice policy for a specific school (real or hypothetical). Be specific, practical, and aligned with restorative principles.

SCHOOL RESTORATIVE JUSTICE POLICY DRAFT

School Name: ______________________________

Date: ______________________________

---

1. VISION AND PHILOSOPHY

Our Vision for School Community:

What We Believe About Discipline:

Restorative Justice Principles We Affirm:

☐ Harm is to people and relationships, not just rules
☐ Those affected by harm should participate in resolution
☐ Accountability means taking responsibility and making amends
☐ Community plays a role in healing and prevention
☐ All people have dignity and capacity for growth

2. SCOPE AND PURPOSE

This policy applies to:

☐ All students
☐ All staff
☐ All school settings (classrooms, hallways, cafeteria, grounds, events)
☐ All incidents involving harm to persons or relationships

Purposes of Restorative Practices in Our School:

1. ____________________
2. ____________________
3. ____________________
4. ____________________

3. TYPES OF RESTORATIVE PRACTICES

Practice	Description	When Used
Community-Building Circles		
Curriculum Circles		

Practice	Description	When Used
Restorative Conversations		
Problem-Solving Circles		
Conflict Resolution Circles		
Re-Entry Circles		
Staff Circles		

4. REFERRAL PROCESS

Who can refer to restorative justice?

☐ Teachers
☐ Administrators
☐ Counselors
☐ Students (self-referral)
☐ Parents
☐ Other: _______________

Referral form includes:

- Date of referral
- Names of those involved
- Brief description of incident

- Previous interventions attempted
- Any safety concerns

Referral coordinator: ___________________________

Timeline for response: Within _______ school days

---

5. CASE ELIGIBILITY AND SCREENING

Restorative justice is appropriate when:

- The person causing harm acknowledges at least some responsibility
- All parties voluntarily consent to participate
- There is no immediate safety threat that cannot be managed
- Parties are emotionally ready (or can become ready with support)

Restorative justice may not be appropriate when:

- There is an ongoing threat of serious violence
- A party is unable to participate voluntarily (coercion)
- A party is in acute crisis and cannot engage
- The case involves certain legal requirements (mandatory reporting, etc.)

Screening process:

---

6. FACILITATOR REQUIREMENTS

Facilitators will:

- Complete initial training (minimum ____ hours)
- Participate in ongoing professional development
- Receive regular supervision
- Adhere to ethical guidelines
- Maintain confidentiality

Facilitators may be:

☐ Teachers
☐ Counselors
☐ Administrators
☐ Support staff
☐ Trained peer facilitators (with adult co-facilitator)
☐ Community volunteers

Co-facilitation is encouraged when:

7. CIRCLE PROCEDURES

Preparation:

- Individual meetings with each participant
- Explain process and answer questions
- Assess readiness and address concerns
- Discuss ground rules
- Confirm voluntary participation

Opening:

- Welcome and gratitude
- Purpose statement
- Ground rules review
- Opening ritual or centering
- Introductions/check-in

Sharing:

- Talking piece passes
- Each person shares experience and impact
- No interruption or cross-talk
- Facilitator validates contributions

Discussion:

- Explore harm more deeply
- Identify needs
- Generate options
- Build toward agreement

Agreement:

- Summarize proposed actions
- Ensure specificity (who, what, when)
- Document in writing
- Sign by all parties

Closing:

- Invite reflections
- Express gratitude
- Closing ritual
- Clarify follow-up

---

8. AGREEMENTS

Restorative agreements may include:

- Apology (verbal or written)
- Restitution
- Community service
- Behavioral commitments
- Educational components
- Restorative projects
- Other: ______________

Agreements must be:

- Specific
- Achievable
- Relevant to the harm
- Time-bound
- Agreed by all parties

Agreements are documented and signed by:

- Person causing harm
- Person harmed

- Facilitator
- Other: _____________

---

9. FOLLOW-UP AND MONITORING

Follow-up will occur:

- ☐ At ____ days
- ☐ At ____ days
- ☐ At ____ days
- ☐ Other: _____________

Follow-up may include:

- Check-in meetings
- Progress reports
- Follow-up circle
- Celebration of completion

If agreements are not fulfilled:

---

10. CONFIDENTIALITY

What is confidential:

- What is shared in circles
- Facilitator notes (with exceptions)

Exceptions to confidentiality:

- Threat of serious harm to self or others
- Disclosure of unreported child abuse
- Court order
- Other: ______________

Confidentiality is explained to participants:

- During preparation
- At circle opening
- In written materials

11. TRAINING AND PROFESSIONAL DEVELOPMENT

All staff receive:

- Introduction to restorative philosophy
- Overview of school policy and procedures
- Basic restorative language and practices
- Role in supporting restorative culture

Facilitators receive:

- Comprehensive initial training (_____ hours)
- Topics: principles, skills, process, trauma-informed practice, cultural competence, ethics
- Practice and feedback

- Co-facilitation with mentor

Ongoing professional development:

- Monthly peer learning group
- Quarterly advanced training
- Annual refresher
- Access to resources and support

12. STUDENT AND FAMILY ENGAGEMENT

Students will:

- Learn about restorative practices in age-appropriate ways
- Have opportunities to participate in community-building circles
- Be invited to serve as peer facilitators (with training)
- Have voice in restorative program development

Families will:

- Receive information about restorative approaches
- Be invited to participate in restorative processes involving their children
- Have opportunities for input and feedback
- Be supported in understanding restorative philosophy

13. DATA COLLECTION AND EVALUATION

Data to collect:

- Number and types of restorative interventions
- Participant satisfaction

- Agreement completion rates
- Impact on suspension/expulsion rates
- Impact on school climate
- Disaggregated by race, gender, disability, etc.

Evaluation methods:

- Participant surveys
- Facilitator reflections
- Review of school discipline data
- Focus groups
- Annual report

Use of findings:

- Program improvement
- Reporting to stakeholders
- Identifying training needs
- Celebrating successes

14. ROLES AND RESPONSIBILITIES

Role	Responsibilities
Principal	
Restorative Justice Coordinator	
Facilitators	

Role	Responsibilities
Teachers	
Counselors	
Students	
Families	
Community Partners	

---

15. POLICY REVIEW AND REVISION

This policy will be reviewed:

- ☐ Annually
- ☐ Every _____ years
- ☐ As needed

Review process includes input from:

- Students
- Staff
- Families

- Community partners

Revisions will be communicated to all stakeholders.

---

16. APPROVAL

Policy developed by: ______________________________

Date: ______________________________

Approved by: ______________________________

Date: ______________________________

Effective date: ______________________________

Reflection Questions on Policy Draft

1. What part of this policy was easiest to write? What was most challenging?

---

2. How does this policy reflect restorative principles? Where might it fall short?

3. What resistance might this policy face from staff? From students? From families? How would you address it?

4. What resources would be needed to implement this policy effectively?

5. How would you measure whether this policy is working?

6. What would success look like in three years?

7. What lessons do indigenous justice systems offer modern schools? Consider: role of elders, circle process, community involvement, holistic healing, interconnectedness.

Circle Practice: "My Best School Experience"

Purpose: To connect with positive experiences of learning and community, building vision for restorative schools.

Time: 45–60 minutes

Materials: Talking piece, comfortable seating

Opening (5 minutes):

- Welcome participants.
- Remind of confidentiality.
- Introduce the prompt: "Share a positive memory from your school experience—a time when you felt safe, supported, engaged, or connected. What made that experience possible?"

Check-In Round (10 minutes):

- Pass the talking piece. Each person shares their name and one word about how they're arriving.

Sharing Round (20–30 minutes):

- Pass the talking piece. Each person who wishes responds to the prompt.
- Allow silence between speakers.
- No cross-talk or response.

Reflection Round (10 minutes):

- Pass the talking piece. Each person shares: "What made those positive experiences possible? How can we create more of those conditions in schools?"

Closing (5 minutes):

- Thank participants.
- Note the themes that emerged.
- Close with a moment of silence.

Facilitator Notes for Chapter 10

Before the Session:

1. **Read Chapter 10 thoroughly.** Understand the unique application of restorative justice in schools, including the pyramid model and types of circles.
2. **Prepare school scenarios.** Have copies of the three scenarios for small group work.
3. **Gather resources.** If possible, bring examples of actual school restorative policies or circle scripts.
4. **Consider your audience.** If participants are educators, focus on practical classroom application. If they are community members, focus on understanding school contexts.

Session Outline (3–3.5 hours):

Segment	Time	Activity
Opening	10 min	Welcome, check-in, review objectives
Key Concepts	20 min	Present school as covenantal community, pyramid model, types of circles
Scenario 1: Bullying	25 min	Small group design restorative response
Share Scenario 1	10 min	Groups share key elements
Scenario 2: Disruption	20 min	Small group design restorative response
Scenario 3: Teacher-Student	20 min	Small group design restorative response
Break	10 min	

Segment	Time	Activity
Proactive Circle Design	15 min	Individual design of community-building circle
Responding to Resistance	15 min	Practice addressing staff concerns
Policy Draft Introduction	15 min	Review policy template; begin drafting
Circle Practice	20 min	"My Best School Experience"
Closing & Assignment	5 min	Review policy draft assignment

Key Teaching Points:

1. **Restorative justice in schools is both proactive and responsive.** Community-building circles prevent problems; response circles address them when they occur.
2. **Schools are communities, not just institutions.** Relationships matter. Discipline should strengthen, not sever, relationships.

3. **Students should be partners, not just recipients.** Peer facilitation and student voice are essential.
4. **Policy matters.** Without clear policy, restorative practices remain dependent on individual champions and don't survive leadership changes.
5. **Trauma-informed practice is essential in schools.** Many students have experienced trauma. Circles must be safe.

Common Questions:

- **Q: "How do we find time for circles?"** A: Circles can be integrated into existing structures—advisory periods, morning meetings, class meetings. Prevention saves time spent on discipline later.
- **Q: "What about students who refuse to participate?"** A: Voluntariness applies. Alternative consequences may be needed. But skilled facilitators can often engage resistant students through preparation.
- **Q: "Does this work with serious incidents?"** A: Yes, with proper preparation and facilitation. Even suspension can be preceded or followed by a re-entry circle.
- **Q: "What if parents don't support it?"** A: Parent education is essential. Involve parents in policy development. Communicate regularly about restorative approaches.
- **Q: "How do we train all staff?"** A: Start with a core team, then expand. Use staff meetings for ongoing learning. Celebrate successes.

After the Session:

- Collect policy drafts for feedback.

- Connect participants with school restorative justice resources.
- Prepare for Chapter 11 on restorative justice in the workplace.

Personal Journal: Chapter 10

Date: ______________

The most important thing I learned about restorative justice in schools:

____

____

A school experience that shaped me:

____

____

How I would implement restorative practices in a school:

____

____

A challenge I anticipate and how I might address it:

A question I'm still holding:

Key Terms Glossary for Chapter 10

Term	Definition
Covenantal Community	A community bound by mutual commitment and shared purpose
Restorative Pyramid	Three-tiered model: universal prevention, targeted intervention, intensive response
Community-Building Circles	Proactive circles to build relationships and trust

Term	Definition
Re-Entry Circles	Circles welcoming students back after absence or suspension
Peer Facilitator	Student trained to co-facilitate restorative circles
Zero-Tolerance	Policies mandating predetermined consequences regardless of circumstances
School-to-Prison Pipeline	Policies and practices that push students out of school and into justice system
Positive Behavioral Interventions and Supports (PBIS)	Framework for teaching and reinforcing positive behavior; can integrate restorative practices

"*Restorative justice circles in schools are not merely interventions for addressing problems but practices for forming community. They teach students how to be in relationship—how to listen, how to speak, how to take responsibility, how to make amends, how to forgive, how to be restored.*" — Dr. Maxwell Shimba

CHAPTER 11

Restorative Justice Circles in the Workplace

Learning Objectives

By completing this chapter, you will be able to:

- **Understand the unique dynamics** of workplace conflicts and their impact on individuals and organizations
- **Identify the multiple purposes** of restorative circles in workplace settings
- **Analyze how unresolved conflict** affects productivity, morale, and organizational health

- **Design and facilitate** restorative responses to workplace grievances and conflicts
- **Develop workplace policies** that embed restorative principles into organizational culture
- **Apply restorative approaches** to improve communication, collaboration, and accountability

---

Key Concepts from Chapter 11

1. The Workplace as Covenantal Community

The workplace is more than a location where labor is exchanged for wages; it is a community where human beings spend the majority of their waking hours, where they form relationships, where they experience both fulfillment and frustration, where they contribute to something larger than themselves.

Theological Foundation: The creation narrative presents work as part of humanity's original vocation: "The Lord God took the man and put him in the Garden of Eden to work it and take care of it" (Genesis 2:15). Work is not a curse but a gift—a participation in God's creative and sustaining activity. The prophets denounce exploitation in the workplace. Paul calls believers to work "with all your heart, as working for the Lord" (Colossians 3:23).

2. Why Workplace Conflict Matters

Dimension	Impact of Unresolved Conflict
Individual	Stress, anxiety, depression, physical symptoms, burnout
Relational	Eroded trust, damaged relationships, isolation
Team	Reduced collaboration, silos, loss of collective efficacy
Organizational	Decreased productivity, increased turnover, damaged culture
Financial	Costs of absenteeism, turnover, litigation, lost productivity

3. The Five Purposes of Restorative Circles in the Workplace

Purpose	Description
Conflict Resolution	Addressing specific disputes between employees, teams, or managers

Purpose	Description
Improved Communication	Breaking down barriers; teaching active listening and constructive feedback
Relationship Building	Strengthening the fabric of workplace community
Enhanced Collaboration	Building trust and shared purpose across functions and levels
Promoting Accountability	Creating conditions for employees to take responsibility and make amends

4. Common Workplace Applications

Application	Description
Interpersonal Conflicts	Disputes between colleagues, personality clashes
Team Conflicts	Dysfunction within or between teams

Application	Description
Manager-Employee Conflicts	Power dynamics, communication breakdowns, perceived unfairness
Grievances	Formal complaints that may benefit from restorative process
Workplace Harassment	When appropriate, survivor-centered restorative responses
Organizational Change	Addressing stress and conflict during restructuring
Re-entry after Leave	Welcoming employees back after extended absence
Termination/Exit	Restorative closure when employment ends

5. Legal Framework for Workplace Restorative Justice

Consideration	Implication
Employment at Will	Default rule; exceptions for discrimination, retaliation
Anti-Discrimination Laws	Title VII, ADA, ADEA—restorative justice must not circumvent protections
Alternative Dispute Resolution	ADR increasingly used; must respect employee rights
Confidentiality	Careful management of sensitive information
Due Process	Employees must have fair opportunity to be heard
Union Considerations	Collective bargaining agreements may affect restorative processes

6. Psychological Dimensions of Workplace Conflict

Concept	Application
Workplace Stress	Conflict increases stress; restorative processes reduce it
Job Satisfaction	Strongly influenced by colleague relationships
Organizational Commitment	Enhanced by fair, respectful processes
Psychological Safety	Belief that one can speak up without fear—essential for healthy workplace
Procedural Justice	Fair processes (voice, neutrality, respect, trust) increase acceptance of outcomes

7. Restorative Cycles in the Workplace

Biological Process	Workplace Parallel
Inflammatory Phase	Acknowledgment of conflict; naming the harm

Biological Process	Workplace Parallel
Proliferative Phase	Active reconstruction through dialogue and problem-solving
Remodeling Phase	Strengthening new patterns through follow-up and support

Reflection Questions

1. How does unresolved conflict affect productivity and morale?

Think of a workplace conflict you have experienced or witnessed. Consider:

- How did it affect the individuals involved? (stress, focus, engagement, health)

- How did it affect the team? (collaboration, trust, communication)

- How did it affect the organization? (productivity, turnover, culture)

- What was the cost—human and financial—of leaving this conflict unresolved?

2. Think of a time when you experienced fair treatment in a workplace conflict. What made it fair?

3. Think of a time when you experienced unfair treatment. What was missing?

4. The chapter describes the workplace as a "covenantal community." What would this mean in your workplace? What would need to change?

5. What fears might employees have about participating in a restorative circle? How could those be addressed?

6. What fears might managers have? How could those be addressed?

7. How might restorative justice affect workplace culture beyond resolving specific conflicts?

8. What lessons do indigenous justice systems offer modern workplaces? Consider: community involvement, circle process, focus on relationship repair, role of respected elders/leaders, holistic approach to harm.

Exercise 1: Cost of Conflict Calculator

Purpose: To quantify the impact of unresolved workplace conflict, building the case for restorative approaches.

Instructions: For a specific workplace conflict you know about (or a hypothetical), estimate the costs below.

Cost Category	Estimated Impact	Notes
Direct Time (hours spent on conflict by all parties)		
Management Time (hours spent addressing conflict)		
HR Time (hours spent on investigation, documentation)		
Lost Productivity (% decrease × salary × duration)		
Absenteeism (days lost × daily cost)		
Turnover (if someone leaves: recruitment, training, lost knowledge)		
Health Costs (stress-related illness, insurance)		

Cost Category	Esti-mated Impact	Notes
Legal Costs (if applicable)		
Morale Impact (hard to quantify but real)		
Reputation Impact (hard to quantify but real)		

Total Estimated Cost: $____________

Reflection: How might a restorative circle, costing perhaps a few hours of facilitated time, compare to these costs?

Exercise 2: Workplace Conflict Scenarios

Purpose: To practice designing restorative responses to common workplace conflicts.

Instructions: For each scenario, complete the response template.

SCENARIO A: INTERPERSONAL CONFLICT

Background:

Two colleagues, Priya and James, work in the same department. They have been in conflict for months. Priya feels James takes credit for her ideas in meetings and undermines her work. James feels Priya is overly sensitive and refuses to collaborate. Their conflict is affecting team morale, and other team members feel caught in the middle. Their manager has tried talking to them individually, but the situation is worsening.

Those Affected:

Stakeholder	How Affected
Priya	
James	
Other team members	
Their manager	

Stakeholder	How Affected
The department	

Restorative Response Design:

1. Preparation Needed:

Who needs individual meetings? What concerns might they have?

2. Circle Participants:

Who should be included?

3. Opening:

What ground rules are essential?

How will you state the purpose?

4. Sharing Prompts:

For Priya: ______________________________

For James: ______________________________

For others: ______________________________

5. Discussion Questions:

What needs to be explored?

6. Possible Agreement Elements:

Action	Responsible Party	Timeline

7. Follow-Up Plan:

SCENARIO B: MANAGER-EMPLOYEE CONFLICT

Background:

David manages a team of five. One team member, Sarah, has complained that David micromanages her, doesn't trust her judgment, and publicly corrects her in ways that feel humiliating. David says Sarah is defensive, doesn't take feedback well, and has missed several deadlines. Their relationship has deteriorated to the point where they barely speak. Sarah is considering quitting. David is frustrated and doesn't know what to do.

Those Affected:

Stakeholder	How Affected
Sarah	
David	
Other team members	
HR	
The organization	

Restorative Response Design:

1. Preparation Needed:

Who needs individual meetings? What concerns might they have?

---

2. Circle Participants:

Who should be included? (Consider: HR representative? Support persons?)

---

3. Opening:

What ground rules are essential given the power imbalance?

How will you state the purpose?

---

4. Sharing Prompts:

For Sarah: ____

For David: ____

5. Discussion Questions:

What needs to be explored? (Consider: communication styles, expectations, feedback methods, trust)

6. Possible Agreement Elements:

Action	Responsible Party	Timeline

7. Follow-Up Plan:

SCENARIO C: TEAM CONFLICT

Background:

A marketing team of eight people is deeply divided. Four members want to pursue a bold new direction; four want to stick with proven strategies. The conflict has become personal, with each side questioning the other's competence and commitment.

Meetings are tense and unproductive. Projects are falling behind. The team leader, Maria, feels helpless.

Those Affected:

Stakeholder	How Affected
Each team member	
Maria (team leader)	
Other departments who depend on marketing	
The organization	

Restorative Response Design:

1. Preparation Needed:

Who needs individual meetings? What concerns might they have?

2. Circle Participants:

Should the whole team participate? Should Maria facilitate or have an outside facilitator?

3. Opening:

What ground rules are essential?

How will you state the purpose?

4. Sharing Prompts:

What questions will help each person share their perspective?

5. Discussion Questions:

What needs to be explored? (Consider: values, goals, fears, assumptions)

6. Possible Agreement Elements:

Action	Responsible Party	Timeline

7. Follow-Up Plan:

Exercise 3: Communication Patterns Analysis

Purpose: To identify communication patterns that contribute to workplace conflict and practice restorative alternatives.

Instructions: For each problematic pattern, identify the impact and suggest a restorative alternative.

Problematic Pattern	Example	Impact	Restorative Alternative
Blaming	"You always miss deadlines."		
Interrupting	Cutting someone off mid-sentence		
Dismissing	"You're overreacting."		
Speaking for others	"Everyone thinks you're difficult."		
Assuming intent	"You did that just to embarrass me."		
Defensiveness	Immediately justifying without listening		
Stonewalling	Silence, withdrawal, refusal to engage		

Problematic Pattern	Example	Impact	Restorative Alternative
Generalizing	"You never listen." / "You always do this."		

Exercise 4: Accountability Scenarios

Purpose: To practice facilitating conversations where employees take responsibility for harm.

Instructions: For each scenario, write what you would say to help the person move toward genuine accountability.

Scenario 1: A manager who publicly humiliated an employee

The manager says in preparation: "I was just giving feedback. She's too sensitive. I've been doing this for 20 years and no one else has complained."

How do you respond?

Scenario 2: An employee who spread rumors about a colleague

The employee says: "I was just joking around. Everyone does it. I didn't mean any harm."

How do you respond?

Scenario 3: A team member who consistently fails to deliver on commitments

The employee says: "I've been really busy. Everyone understands. It's not a big deal."

How do you respond?

Scenario 4: A leader who took credit for a subordinate's work

The leader says: "I provided guidance and oversight. The success reflects on the whole team, including my leadership."

How do you respond?

Exercise 5: Designing a Workplace Restorative Policy

Purpose: To develop key elements of a workplace restorative justice policy.

Instructions: Draft each section for your workplace (real or hypothetical).

WORKPLACE RESTORATIVE JUSTICE POLICY DRAFT

Organization: ______________________________

____

1. Vision and Philosophy

What do we believe about conflict, accountability, and community in our workplace?

____

____

____

2. Scope

What types of conflicts or concerns are appropriate for restorative process?

____

____

3. Referral Process

How do employees access restorative processes? Who can refer?

4. Voluntary Participation

How will we ensure participation is voluntary and informed?

5. Facilitators

Who will facilitate? What training will they have?

6. Confidentiality

What is confidential? What exceptions apply?

7. Relationship to Formal Processes

How does restorative justice relate to HR processes, grievance procedures, and legal requirements?

8. Agreements

What can restorative agreements include? How will they be documented and monitored?

9. Follow-Up

How will we ensure agreements are kept and relationships continue to improve?

10. Evaluation

How will we know if restorative processes are working?

Practical Exercise: Simulate a Workplace Grievance Circle

Purpose: To practice facilitating a restorative circle in response to a workplace grievance.

Time: 60–75 minutes

Format: Small groups of 6-8 people. One person serves as facilitator. Others play roles. After the simulation, debrief thoroughly.

SCENARIO FOR SIMULATION

Background:

A mid-sized nonprofit organization has been experiencing tension between two departments—Programs and Development. The conflict came to a head when a grant proposal was submitted late, potentially losing a significant funding opportunity. Each department blames the other.

The Incident:

A major grant proposal was due on Friday. The Programs department was responsible for providing program narratives and data. The Development department was responsible for writing the proposal and submitting it. The Programs director, Marcus, sent the materials late Thursday afternoon with a note that he'd been too busy to get it sooner. The Development director, Elena, was frustrated but worked late to complete the proposal. However, in her rush, she missed a formatting requirement, and the proposal was rejected. Elena believes if Marcus had sent materials earlier, she would have had time to review properly. Marcus believes Elena should have checked the requirements earlier.

The Aftermath:

The conflict has escalated. In a staff meeting, Elena said publicly, "If Programs had done their job on time, we wouldn't have lost this funding." Marcus responded, "If Development knew what they were doing, they'd have caught the error." Other staff are taking sides. Trust between departments is broken. The Executive Director, Pat, has asked for a restorative circle to address the conflict before it damages the organization further.

Roles:

Role	Description	Key Concerns
Marcus	Programs Director	Feels blamed unfairly; believes Elena should have checked requirements earlier; understaffed and overworked
Elena	Development	Feels Marcus's lateness caused the problem; believes he doesn't respect her department's deadlines

Role	Description	Key Concerns
	Director	
Pat	Executive Director	Wants the conflict resolved; concerned about organizational culture and future funding
Jamal	Programs Staff	Works for Marcus; feels his team is being scapegoated; tense with Development colleagues
Leah	Development Staff	Works for Elena; frustrated with Programs' delays; wants accountability
Taylor	HR Representative	Ensuring process is fair; concerned about legal implications

Role	Description	Key Concerns
Facilitator	(one person)	Guides the circle process

Preparation (10 minutes before circle simulation):

- Facilitator meets briefly (2-3 minutes each) with each participant to explain process and assess readiness.
- Participants get into character.

Circle Simulation (45 minutes):

- **Opening** (5 min): Welcome, purpose, ground rules, check-in
- **Sharing** (15 min): Talking piece passes; each shares their experience of the conflict and its impact
- **Discussion** (15 min): Facilitated dialogue exploring underlying issues, needs, and possible solutions
- **Agreement** (5 min): Identify specific commitments
- **Closing** (5 min): Reflections, gratitude

Debrief Questions (15 minutes):

For the facilitator:

- What was challenging about facilitating this workplace conflict?

- How did you handle the power dynamics? The emotions? The blame?
- What would you do differently?

For participants:

- How did the facilitator's presence affect the process?
- What did the facilitator do that was helpful?
- What could have been done differently?

For observers:

- What did you notice about the dynamics?
- What restorative principles were evident? What was missing?

Circle Practice: "A Workplace Experience That Shaped Me"

Purpose: To connect personal workplace experiences with restorative principles.

Time: 45–60 minutes

Materials: Talking piece, comfortable seating

Opening (5 minutes):

- Welcome participants.
- Remind of confidentiality.
- Introduce the prompt: "Share a workplace experience that shaped how you think about conflict, accountability, or community. This could be positive or negative—a time when conflict was handled well or poorly, when you felt

valued or devalued, when you learned something important about work relationships."

Check-In Round (10 minutes):

- Pass the talking piece. Each person shares their name and one word about how they're arriving.

Sharing Round (20–30 minutes):

- Pass the talking piece. Each person who wishes responds to the prompt.
- Allow silence between speakers.
- No cross-talk or response.

Reflection Round (10 minutes):

- Pass the talking piece. Each person shares: "What did I learn from hearing these workplace stories?"

Closing (5 minutes):

- Thank participants.
- Note the themes that emerged.
- Close with a moment of silence.

Facilitator Notes for Chapter 11

Before the Session:

1. **Read Chapter 11 thoroughly.** Understand the unique dynamics of workplace conflicts and the legal framework.
2. **Prepare for the simulation.** This is the most comp ex exercise. Brief role-players in advance. Consider having co-facilitators.

3. **Gather workplace examples.** If possible, bring real (anonymized) examples of workplace conflicts and restorative responses.
4. **Consider your audience.** If participants are from the same workplace, be sensitive to actual conflicts that may exist.

Session Outline (3–3.5 hours):

Segment	Time	Activity
Opening	10 min	Welcome, check-in, review objectives
Key Concepts	20 min	Present workplace as community, purposes of circles, legal framework
Reflection Questions	15 min	Individual writing on conflict's impact
Cost of Conflict	10 min	Calculate costs of unresolved conflict
Scenario Analysis	30 min	Small groups work on 2-3 scenarios

Segment	Time	Activity
Break	10 min	
Communication Patterns	15 min	Identify and practice alternatives
Accountability Scenarios	15 min	Practice responses to defensiveness
Simulation Setup	10 min	Assign roles, prepare for grievance circle
Simulation	45 min	Conduct workplace grievance circle
Debrief Simulation	15 min	Discuss learning
Policy Draft	10 min	Begin drafting policy elements

Segment	Time	Activity
Circle Prac-tice	15 min	"A Workplace Experience That Shaped Me"
Closing & Assignment	5 min	Review policy draft assignment

Key Teaching Points:

1. **Workplace conflict is costly.** Financially, relationally, and organizationally. Restorative justice is an investment, not an expense.
2. **Power dynamics are real.** Manager-employee conflicts require careful attention to ensure safety and voice.
3. **Voluntariness can be complicated.** Employees may feel pressure to participate. Facilitators must ensure genuine choice.
4. **Confidentiality must be clear.** What is shared in circle stays in circle, with clear exceptions.
5. **Follow-up is essential.** Workplace relationships need ongoing attention, not just one-time fixes.

Common Questions:

- **Q: "What if someone refuses to participate?"** A: Voluntariness applies. Alternative HR processes may be needed. But skilled preparation can often address reluctance.

- **Q: "What about harassment or discrimination claims?"**
  A: Restorative justice can be used alongside formal processes, but must not circumvent legal protections. Survivor safety is paramount.
- **Q: "How do we handle power imbalances between managers and employees?"**
  A: Preparation, support persons, skilled facilitation, and sometimes separate meetings. The facilitator must actively protect against domination.
- **Q: "What if the conflict involves the CEO or senior leadership?"**
  A: External facilitators may be needed. Power dynamics are even more significant. Leadership must model accountability.
- **Q: "How do we measure success?"**
  A: Participant satisfaction, agreement completion, improved relationships, reduced future conflicts, climate surveys.

After the Session:

- Collect policy drafts for feedback.
- Follow up on simulation debrief.
- Prepare for Chapter 12 on restorative justice in the criminal justice system.

Personal Journal: Chapter 11

Date: ______________

The most important thing I learned about workplace restorative justice:

A workplace experience that shaped me:

How I would handle a workplace conflict restoratively:

A challenge I anticipate and how I might address it:

A question I'm still holding:

Key Terms Glossary for Chapter 11

Term	Definition
Covenantal Community	A workplace bound by mutual commitment and shared purpose, not just contract
Procedural Justice	Fairness of process (voice, neutrality, respect, trust)
Psychological Safety	Belief that one can speak up without fear of negative consequences
Social Capital	Networks of relationships, trust, and reciprocity
Collective Efficacy	Shared belief that the group can solve problems together
Alternative Dispute Resolution (ADR)	Processes (mediation, arbitration, restorative justice) as alternatives to litigation

Term	Definition
Employment at Will	Default rule allowing termination for any non-discriminatory reason
Vicarious Trauma	Transformation of helper's inner experience through empathic engagement
Compassion Fatigue	Emotional exhaustion from caring for others' suffering

---

"The workplace is more than a location where labor is exchanged for wages; it is a community where human beings spend the majority of their waking hours, where they form relationships, where they experience both fulfillment and frustration, where they contribute to something larger than themselves." — Dr. Maxwell Shimba

CHAPTER 12

Restorative Justice Circles in the Criminal Justice System

Learning Objectives

By completing this chapter, you will be able to:

- **Understand the role** of restorative justice within the criminal justice system
- **Identify the key functions** of restorative circles for victims, offenders, and communities
- **Analyze ethical questions** about the appropriate scope of restorative justice

- **Assess the suitability** of restorative processes for different types of offenses
- **Apply restorative principles** to cases involving serious and violent harm
- **Understand the legal frameworks** that govern restorative justice in criminal contexts
- **Design restorative responses** that honor victims' needs while holding offenders accountable

Key Concepts from Chapter 12

1. Justice as Covenantal Faithfulness

The criminal justice system stands at the intersection of society's most profound questions about harm, accountability, and restoration. The biblical tradition offers a distinctive vision of justice that stands in sharp contrast to the retributive assumptions dominating Western legal systems.

Theological Foundation: In Hebrew Scripture, justice (*mishpat*) and righteousness (*tsedaqah*) are not primarily about punishment but about putting things right, restoring relationships, creating conditions for flourishing. The prophets call for justice that protects the vulnerable: "Learn to do right; seek justice. Defend the oppressed" (Isaiah 1:17). Paul declares that "God was in Christ reconciling the world to himself, not counting people's sins against them" (2 Corinthians 5:19). Divine justice is fundamentally reconciliatory.

2. The Five Functions of Restorative Justice in Criminal Justice

Function	Description
Repairing Harm	Addressing the material, emotional, and relational consequences of crime
Fostering Accountability	Active responsibility—confronting human consequences, acknowledging harm, making amends
Supporting Rehabilitation	Addressing underlying causes, engaging community support, enabling change
Reducing Recidivism	Breaking cycles of reoffending through empathy, reintegration, and social bonds
Empowering Victims	Giving voice, validation, and participation in determining outcomes

3. Repairing Harm: The Heart of Restorative Justice

Theological Foundation: Joel speaks God's promise: "I will repay you for the years the locusts have eaten" (Joel 2:25). The Jubilee (Leviticus 25) provides the comprehensive model—debts forgiven, land returned, slaves liberated. Zacchaeus models restorative repair: "If I have cheated anybody, I will pay back four times the amount" (Luke 19:8).

Legal Framework: The UN Declaration of Basic Principles of Justice for Victims (1985) affirms victims' right to restitution. Many jurisdictions now require restitution as part of criminal sentences.

Psychological Research: Victims who receive restitution, apologies, and repair show reduced PTSD symptoms, lower anger and anxiety, and greater satisfaction with justice.

Restorative Cycles Parallel: Repair is the proliferative phase of healing—active reconstruction of damaged tissue.

4. Fostering Accountability

Theological Foundation: Confession (*homologia*) and repentance (*metanoia*)—speaking truth and changing direction. John the Baptist demands "fruit in keeping with repentance" (Luke 3:8).

Legal Framework: Restorative accountability differs from liability for punishment. It requires active engagement in repairing harm, not passive endurance of sanctions.

Psychological Research:

- **Cognitive dissonance** – voluntary acknowledgment creates discomfort motivating change
- **Self-determination theory** – autonomous choice supports internalized motivation
- **Reintegrative shame** – shame focused on behavior, not person, reduces reoffending

5. Supporting Rehabilitation

Theological Foundation: The lost sheep (Luke 15)—the shepherd seeks, finds, and restores. Paul's transformation from persecutor to apostle models radical change.

Legal Framework: Rehabilitation is recognized as a goal of sentencing, though often pursued coercively. Restorative justice offers an alternative based on voluntary engagement and community support.

Psychological Research:

- **Cognitive transformation** – changes in identity, values, worldviews
- **Social bonds** – connections to prosocial networks support desistance
- **Procedural justice** – fair treatment enhances legitimacy and compliance

6. Reducing Recidivism

Theological Foundation: Isaiah's vision of "proclaiming freedom for the captives" (Isaiah 61:1)—release from cycles of offending.

Psychological Research: Meta-analyses demonstrate restorative justice produces significant reductions in reoffending compared to conventional processing. Mechanisms include empathy development, reintegrative shame, and social capital.

7. Empowering Victims

Theological Foundation: The Psalms are filled with victims' cries. God hears the cry of the oppressed (Exodus 3:7). Jesus attends to victims—Bartimaeus, the hemorrhaging woman, the widow of Nain.

Legal Framework: Victims' rights movement has achieved recognition of victims' right to be heard, present, and notified. Restorative justice extends this to meaningful participation in outcomes.

Psychological Research: Voice and validation are consistently associated with victim satisfaction and healing. Closure is facilitated by answers to victims' questions and tangible repair.

8. Restorative Cycles in Criminal Justice

Biological Process	Criminal Justice Parallel
Inflammatory Phase	Acknowledgment of harm through victim testimony
Proliferative Phase	Active repair through restitution, apology, community service
Remodeling Phase	Reintegration and sustained change through follow-up

Ethical Reflection: Should All Crimes Be Eligible for Restorative Justice?

Purpose: To critically examine the appropriate scope of restorative justice in criminal matters.

Instructions: Read the arguments below. Then develop your own position using the reflection questions.

Arguments FOR broad eligibility:

- Restorative justice addresses harm to victims, which occurs in all crimes
- Even serious offenders can experience transformation
- Victims of serious crimes may need restorative processes most
- Conventional justice often fails victims of serious crimes
- Restorative justice has been used successfully in cases of severe violence, including homicide

Arguments AGAINST broad eligibility:

- Some offenders are not capable of genuine accountability
- Victims may be re-traumatized by facing offenders
- Power imbalances may be too severe in some cases (e.g., domestic violence)
- Society's need for denunciation may not be satisfied
- Some crimes may require incapacitation for public safety

Theological Reflection: The thief on the cross (Luke 23:39-43) received mercy in his final moments. Paul, who approved of Stephen's murder, became the apostle to the Gentiles. The Bible suggests no one is beyond the reach of grace. Yet justice also requires protection of the vulnerable and accountability for harm.

Reflection Questions on Eligibility

1. What criteria should determine whether a case is suitable for restorative justice?

☐ Offender acknowledges responsibility
☐ Offender expresses genuine remorse
☐ Victim voluntarily wishes to participate
☐ There is no ongoing threat to victim safety
☐ The offense is non-violent
☐ The offense is violent but victim desires encounter
☐ Other: ____________

Why these criteria?

---

2. Should there be any crimes that are **never** eligible for restorative justice? If so, which ones and why?

---

3. Should restorative justice be available for domestic violence cases? What special considerations would be needed?

---

4. Should restorative justice be available for sexual assault cases? What special considerations would be needed?

5. Should restorative justice be available for homicide cases? How could that work when the victim is deceased?

6. Who should decide whether a case is suitable—judges, prosecutors, victims, facilitators, or some combination?

7. How do you balance the victim's needs, the offender's potential for change, and the community's need for safety?

8. What lessons do indigenous justice systems offer about responding to serious harms? Consider how Maori, First Nations, or Ubuntu traditions address severe offenses.

Case Review: Analyzing a Violent Offense

Purpose: To practice assessing the suitability of restorative justice for a serious case.

Instructions: Read the case below. Complete the analysis template, then make a recommendation about whether restorative justice should be offered.

CASE: Assault with Serious Injury

Background:

Marcus, age 24, was involved in a bar fight that resulted in serious injury to another man, David. The altercation began with an argument that escalated. Marcus threw a punch that caused David to fall and hit his head on the pavement. David suffered a traumatic brain injury and spent three weeks in the hospital. He has permanent cognitive impairment and will require ongoing care. Marcus was charged with aggravated assault and faces 5-15 years in prison.

Marcus's Situation:

Marcus has no prior criminal record. He is employed as a construction worker, supports his younger siblings, and has expressed deep remorse. He says he didn't intend to cause serious harm—he threw one punch in anger and "everything went wrong." He has written a letter of apology to David (which David's family has not seen). He wants to take responsibility but is terrified of prison. He would be willing to participate in restorative justice if David or his family would agree.

David's Situation:

David, age 32, was a teacher before the assault. He is now unable to work, requires full-time care, and will never fully recover. His family is devastated and angry. His wife, Sarah, is now his primary caregiver and is struggling with the physical, emotional, and financial burden. She says she wants Marcus "to rot in prison." David's mother, Rosa, has said she would like to understand why this happened and to tell Marcus what his actions have cost their family, but she doesn't want to cause more pain to Sarah.

Case Analysis Template

1. THE HARM

What was the harm? (Describe the full impact)

Who was affected? (List all direct and indirect victims)

What are the ongoing consequences for each?

2. THE OFFENDER

Has Marcus acknowledged responsibility? To what extent?

Is his remorse genuine? What evidence?

What are his capacities for participation? (emotional, psychological, practical)

What risks does he pose?

3. THE VICTIMS

What are the needs of each affected party?

David: ____________________

Sarah: ____________________

Rosa: ____________________

Other family: ____

Do any victims wish to participate? Under what conditions?

____

What support would they need?

____

____

4. SAFETY CONSIDERATIONS

Are there ongoing safety concerns? What are they?

____

What safeguards would be needed for a restorative process?

____

Is the power imbalance manageable with appropriate safeguards?

____

____

5. RESTORATIVE SUITABILITY ASSESSMENT

Factor	Yes	No	Uncer-tain	Notes
Offender acknowledges responsibility	☐	☐	☐	
Offender expresses genuine remorse	☐	☐	☐	
Victim(s) voluntarily willing to participate	☐	☐	☐	
Safety can be adequately managed	☐	☐	☐	
No ongoing threat to victim safety	☐	☐	☐	
Offender has capacity to participate	☐	☐	☐	
Victim(s) have adequate support	☐	☐	☐	

Factor	Yes	No	Uncer-tain	Notes
Community has resources to support process	☐	☐	☐	

6. RECOMMENDATION

Based on your analysis, should restorative justice be offered in this case? Why or why not?

If yes, what conditions or safeguards would be necessary?

If no, what alternative responses might address victims' needs?

Exercise 1: Restorative Justice in Juvenile vs. Adult Systems

Purpose: To compare restorative applications in juvenile and adult criminal justice.

Instructions: Complete the table comparing juvenile and adult applications.

Dimension	Juvenile Justice	Adult Justice
Developmental considerations		
Types of offenses typically eligible		
Role of family		
Common restorative models		

Dimension	Juvenile Justice	Adult Justice
Potential outcomes		
Challenges		
Evidence of effectiveness		

Reflection:

Why has restorative justice been more widely adopted in juvenile than adult systems?

What can adult systems learn from juvenile restorative justice?

Exercise 2: Victim-Offender Dialogue Preparation

Purpose: To practice preparing victims and offenders for dialogue in serious cases.

Instructions: For the case above (Marcus and David), write preparation questions and considerations for each party.

PREPARING THE VICTIM'S FAMILY (Sarah and/or Rosa)

What do they need to understand about the restorative process?

What fears might they have? How would you address them?

What questions might they want to ask Marcus?

What would they need to feel safe?

What support might they need during and after?

PREPARING THE OFFENDER (Marcus)

What does he need to understand about the restorative process?

What fears might he have? How would you address them?

What does he need to understand about the impact of his actions?

What would genuine accountability look like in this case?

What support might he need during and after?

Exercise 3: Designing a Re-Entry Circle

Purpose: To practice designing restorative processes for offenders returning to community after incarceration.

Instructions: Design a re-entry circle for Marcus, assuming he serves a prison sentence and is being released.

Background for Re-Entry:

Marcus served 5 years in prison. He participated in anger management, completed his GED, and has been a model prisoner. He is being released on parole. He has no job, no housing, and his relationships with family are strained. He wants to rebuild his life but faces significant barriers.

Re-Entry Circle Design:

Purpose of the re-entry circle:

Who should participate?

Participant	Role/Contribution
Marcus	
Parole officer	
Family member	
Community supporter	
Employer (potential)	
Service provider	
Other:	

Preparation needed for each participant:

Opening (purpose, ground rules, ritual):

Sharing prompts:

For Marcus: ____

For family: ____

For supporters: ____

Discussion topics:

- Housing: ____
- Employment: ____
- Treatment/support: ____
- Relationships: ____
- Accountability: ____

Agreement elements:

Commit-ment	Responsible Party	Time-line	Support Needed

Follow-up plan:

Exercise 4: Restorative Justice and Mass Incarceration

Purpose: To explore how restorative justice addresses systemic issues in criminal justice.

Reflection Questions:

1. How might widespread implementation of restorative justice affect incarceration rates?

2. What role could restorative justice play in addressing racial and economic disparities in the criminal justice system?

3. How does restorative justice challenge or complement the goals of the prison abolition movement?

4. What would it mean to have a "restorative criminal justice system"? What would need to change?

Circle Practice: "A Time When Justice Mattered"

Purpose: To connect personal experiences with justice to the themes of this chapter.

Time: 45–60 minutes

Materials: Talking piece, comfortable seating

Opening (5 minutes):

- Welcome participants.
- Remind of confidentiality.
- Introduce the prompt: "Share a time when justice—or injustice—deeply affected you or someone you love. This could be your own experience with the legal system, something that happened in your community, or a story that shaped your understanding of justice."

Check-In Round (10 minutes):

- Pass the talking piece. Each person shares their name and one word about how they're arriving.

Sharing Round (20–30 minutes):

- Pass the talking piece. Each person who wishes responds to the prompt.
- Allow silence between speakers.
- No cross-talk or response.

Reflection Round (10 minutes):

- Pass the talking piece. Each person shares: "What did I learn from hearing these stories about what justice requires?"

Closing (5 minutes):

- Thank participants.
- Note the themes that emerged.
- Close with a moment of silence.

Practical Assignment: Restorative Justice and Serious Crime Research

Purpose: To investigate real-world applications of restorative justice in serious cases.

Instructions:

1. Research a restorative justice program that works with serious or violent offenses. Examples:
    - Restorative justice in cases of severe violence (e.g., programs in Norway, Belgium)
    - Victim-offender dialogue in homicide cases (e.g., Texas Department of Criminal Justice)
    - Restorative justice in cases of sexual harm (e.g., RESTORE program in Arizona)
    - Truth and Reconciliation Commission (South Africa)
2. Write a 2-3 page report addressing:
    - What types of cases does the program handle?
    - What is the process?
    - What safeguards are in place?
    - What outcomes have been documented?
    - What challenges has the program faced?
    - What lessons can be learned for restorative justice in serious cases?

Facilitator Notes for Chapter 12

Before the Session:

1. **Read Chapter 12 thoroughly.** This chapter deals with the most serious applications of restorative justice. Be prepared for intense discussions.
2. **Prepare for ethical debate.** The question of eligibility for serious crimes will evoke strong opinions. Create space for respectful disagreement.

3. **Gather resources.** Have information about actual restorative justice programs working with serious offenses.
4. **Be trauma-informed.** Some participants may have personal experience with violent crime. Have support resources available.

Session Outline (3–3.5 hours):

Segment	Time	Activity
Opening	10 min	Welcome, check-in, review objectives
Key Concepts	20 min	Present five functions, legal framework
Ethical Reflection	25 min	Small group discussion on eligibility
Full group share	10 min	Groups report key insights
Case Review	30 min	Analyze Marcus/David case individually or in pairs

Segment	Time	Activity
Break	10 min	
Victim-Offender Preparation	20 min	Practice preparation questions
Juvenile vs. Adult	15 min	Compare systems
Re-Entry Circle Design	20 min	Design re-entry circle
Circle Practice	20 min	"A Time When Justice Mattered"
Closing & Assignment	5 min	Review research assignment

Key Teaching Points:

1. **Restorative justice is not "soft" on crime.** It demands more of offenders—confronting victims, understanding impact, making amends—than passive punishment.

2. **Victims' needs must be central.** Restorative justice should never pressure victims or prioritize offender benefits over victim healing.
3. **Safety is paramount.** In serious cases, rigorous screening, preparation, and safeguards are essential.
4. **Restorative justice can complement, not replace, conventional justice.** Some cases may need both accountability through the system and healing through restorative processes.
5. **No one is beyond hope.** The theological tradition affirms the possibility of transformation, even for those who have caused great harm. But hope must be balanced with protection and accountability.

Common Questions:

- **Q: "Can restorative justice work for murder?"**
  A: Yes, programs exist where victims' family members meet offenders. These are highly sensitive, require extensive preparation, and focus on victim healing.
- **Q: "What about sex offenders?"**
  A: Some programs work with sexual harm, with rigorous safeguards. Not all cases are suitable; offender must acknowledge responsibility and victims must be fully supported.
- **Q: "Doesn't this just give offenders what they want—avoiding prison?"**
  A: Restorative justice is not about avoiding consequences. Offenders may still serve prison time. The focus is on repairing harm, not reducing punishment.
- **Q: "What if the victim wants revenge, not restoration?"**
  A: That's their right. Restorative justice is offered, not

imposed. Some victims need time; some never want encounter. Their choice must be honored.

- **Q: "How do we measure success in serious cases?"**
  A: Victim satisfaction, offender accountability, community healing—not just recidivism. Sometimes a victim's single question answered is success.

After the Session:

- Follow up with anyone who seemed distressed.
- Collect research reports if assigned.
- Prepare for Chapter 13 on cultural and global perspectives.

Personal Journal: Chapter 12

Date: ______________

The most important thing I learned about restorative justice in criminal justice:

My position on eligibility for serious crimes:

A question this chapter raised for me:

How this chapter affected me emotionally:

A question I'm still holding:

Key Terms Glossary for Chapter 12

Term	Definition
Rehabilitation	Process of restoring offenders to productive, law-abiding membership
Recidivism	Reoffending after an intervention
Desistance	Process of ceasing and sustaining cessation from offending
Reintegrative Shame	Shame focused on behavior, with respect for person and pathways to repair
Stigmatizing Shame	Shame focused on person as bad, leading to exclusion
Victim-Offender Dialogue	Facilitated meeting between victim and offender, often in serious cases
Diversion	Redirecting cases from formal prosecution to restorative processes
Pre-Sentencing Circles	Circles conducted before sentencing, with outcomes considered by judge

Term	Definition
Re-Entry Circles	Circles supporting offenders returning to community after incarceration
Truth and Reconciliation Commission	Body addressing historical injustices through truth-telling and acknowledgment

"*The restorative justice movement, which emerged in the 1970s through the work of the Mennonite Central Committee and has since spread throughout the world, represents a recovery of the biblical vision of justice. At its heart is the conviction that crime is first and always harm to people and relationships, and that justice requires repairing that harm.*" — Dr. Maxwell Shimba

CHAPTER 13

Cultural and Global Perspectives on Restorative Justice Circles

Learning Objectives

By completing this chapter, you will be able to:

- **Understand the universality** of restorative principles across diverse cultural contexts
- **Identify and appreciate** indigenous restorative traditions from multiple cultures
- **Recognize the risks** of cultural appropriation and imperialism in restorative justice

- **Develop cultural humility** as a foundation for cross-cultural practice
- **Apply cultural sensitivity** in adapting restorative processes to diverse communities
- **Learn from global examples** of restorative justice in different cultural settings
- **Articulate how restorative justice** can honor both universal principles and cultural particularity

Key Concepts from Chapter 13

1. From Every Nation, Tribe, and Tongue

The book of Revelation presents a vision of the new creation that is breathtaking in its diversity: "a great multitude that no one could count, from every nation, tribe, people and language, standing before the throne" (Revelation 7:9). This vision challenges any understanding of unity that requires uniformity, any conception of truth that denies cultural particularity, any practice of justice that ignores local context.

2. The Universality of Restorative Justice

Foundation	Explanation
Theological	The *imago Dei*—all humans bear God's image, implying universal dignity and universal needs for acknowledgment, accountability, and restoration

Foundation	Explanation
Legal	International human rights frameworks affirm universal rights while respecting cultural particularity (UDHR, UNDRIP, UN Basic Principles)
Psychological	Basic psychological needs (autonomy, competence, relatedness) are universal; procedural justice elements (voice, neutrality, respect, trust) appear across cultures
Biological	Restorative cycles—inflammation, proliferation, remodeling—operate in every human body, regardless of culture

3. Indigenous Restorative Traditions

Culture	Key Concepts	Practices
First Nations (North America)	Sacred circle; interconnectedness; four directions teachings; healing not punishment	Peacemaking circles; elder facilitation; talking piece; spiritual elements; holistic healing

Culture	Key Concepts	Practices
Māori (New Zealand)	*Whakawhanaungatanga* (building relationships); *whakapapa* (genealogy); *utu* (balance)	*Hui* on *marae*; family group conferencing; elder (*kaumatua*) guidance
Ubuntu (Southern Africa)	"A person is a person through persons"; interconnectedness; communal personhood	Community gatherings; consensus-building; restitution; reconciliation ceremonies
Japan	*Wa* (harmony); apology as central; relationship restoration	*Chōtei* (mediation); emphasis on sincere apology; informal processes
European Adaptations	Integration with legal systems; professionalization	Victim-offender mediation; family group conferencing; restorative justice in schools and workplaces

4. Cultural Sensitivity vs. Cultural Imperialism

Cultural Sensitivity	Cultural Imperialism
Learning from local traditions	Imposing foreign models
Engaging cultural leaders	Ignoring local authority
Adapting processes, not principles	Demanding conformity to one model
Humility and openness to correction	Assuming superiority of one's own approach
Reciprocity and partnership	Extraction without acknowledgment
Honoring origins of practices	Appropriation without respect

5. Key Elements for Cross-Cultural Restorative Practice

Element	Description
Learn from local traditions	Before introducing restorative practices, learn about existing traditions of conflict resolution
Engage cultural leaders	Involve elders, religious leaders, and respected community members
Adapt processes, not principles	Adapt form while maintaining core restorative values
Be humble	Recognize limits of one's own cultural understanding
Avoid appropriation	Do not extract cultural practices without understanding, permission, or reciprocity
Build partnerships	Work with cultural communities as partners, not subjects

6. The Danger of Appropriation

Restorative justice draws heavily on indigenous traditions. There is a real danger of:

- Extracting indigenous wisdom without acknowledgment
- Repackaging it in Western forms
- Re-exporting it as a "product"
- Disconnecting practices from their cultural and spiritual roots
- Failing to support indigenous communities and their justice work

Faithful cross-cultural restorative practice requires humility, reciprocity, and genuine partnership.

7. Restorative Cycles Across Cultures

Cycle Phase	Universal Function	Culturally Variable Expression
Inflammatory	Acknowledgment of harm	Formal complaints, public lament, ritualized expression
Proliferative	Active work of repair	Restitution, apology, ritual reconciliation
Remodeling	Strengthening healed relationships	Ongoing support, periodic renewal, commemorative rituals

Cultural Sensitivity Exercise

Purpose: To identify the cultural values that shape your own understanding of justice and to recognize that these values are not universal.

Instructions: Complete each section honestly, reflecting on your own cultural background and how it has shaped your views.

PART A: IDENTIFY YOUR CULTURAL CONTEXT

1. My cultural background(s): (ethnicity, nationality, region, religion, etc.)

---

2. Key values in my culture regarding:

Dimension	Values in My Culture
Individual vs. community (Which is emphasized?)	
Authority and hierarchy (How is power viewed?)	

Dimension	Values in My Culture
Communication style (Direct or indirect? Emotional or reserved?)	
Conflict (Is it avoided, addressed directly, mediated?)	
Time orientation (Past, present, or future focused?)	
Harm and accountability (What does accountability look like?)	
Forgiveness and reconciliation (Are these expected? How are they expressed?)	

PART B: HOW MY CULTURE SHAPES MY VIEW OF JUSTICE

3. When I think of "justice," what images, stories, or experiences come to mind from my culture?

4. What did I learn growing up about how to respond when someone wrongs me?

5. What did I learn about how to respond when I wrong someone else?

6. Who in my culture has authority to resolve disputes? (elders, formal authorities, community, family?)

7. What role does apology play in my culture? What makes an apology meaningful?

PART C: RECOGNIZING MY CULTURAL LENS

8. What assumptions do I make about how conflicts "should" be resolved?

9. What might be surprising or uncomfortable to someone from a different cultural background about my approach to justice?

10. When have I experienced cultural differences in understanding of justice? What happened?

Reflection Questions

1. How can restorative justice avoid cultural imperialism?

Consider:

- What does "cultural imperialism" mean in the context of restorative justice?
- How might well-intentioned restorative practitioners inadvertently impose their cultural assumptions?
- What safeguards can prevent this?

2. The chapter warns against "extracting indigenous wisdom, repackaging it in Western forms, and re-exporting it as a 'product.'" Have you seen examples of this? How can restorative practitioners avoid this pattern?

3. What would genuine partnership with indigenous communities look like in restorative justice work?

4. How do you balance universal restorative principles (inclusivity, voluntariness, respect, etc.) with cultural particularity? When should principles be adapted? When should they be held firm?

5. The chapter describes the Pentecost narrative (Acts 2) as a model for cultural diversity in unity. What does this story teach about cross-cultural understanding?

6. Think of a time when you experienced a cultural misunderstanding. What did you learn? How might that experience inform your restorative practice?

7. What is the difference between cultural sensitivity and cultural appropriation? How can you tell if you're crossing the line?

8. What lessons do indigenous justice systems offer modern societies? Consider: role of elders, circle process, community involvement, holistic healing, interconnectedness, spiritual dimensions, focus on relationships over rules.

Exercise 1: Cultural Values and Justice

Purpose: To explore how different cultural values shape understandings of justice.

Instructions: For each cultural value, consider how it might affect restorative processes. Then reflect on how you would adapt.

Cultural Value	How might this affect restorative justice?	Adaptations a facilitator might make
Collectivism (group identity prioritized over individual)		
Individualism (individual rights and autonomy prioritized)		

Cultural Value	How might this affect restorative justice?	Adaptations a facilitator might make
High power distance (hierarchy accepted and expected)		
Low power distance (equality expected)		
Direct communication (explicit, straightforward)		
Indirect communication (implicit, context-dependent)		
Emotional expressiveness (open display of feelings)		

Cultural Value	How might this affect restorative justice?	Adaptations a facilitator might make
Emotional restraint (control of feelings expected)		
Future orientation (focus on what's ahead)		
Past orientation (focus on tradition and ancestors)		
Present orientation (focus on immediate experience)		

Exercise 2: Indigenous Traditions Comparison

Purpose: To compare restorative traditions from different cultures and identify common elements.

Instructions: Research or recall the traditions discussed in the chapter. Complete the table.

Element	First Nations (North America)	Māori (New Zealand)	Ubuntu (Southern Africa)	Japan
Setting/Space				
Role of elders/leaders				
Spiritual elements				
Decision-making process				
View of harm				

Element	First Nations (North America)	Māori (New Zealand)	Ubuntu (Southern Africa)	Japan
Goal of process				
Role of community				
Role of apology				
Restorative actions				

Common elements across traditions:

Unique elements of each tradition:

What can modern restorative justice learn from each?

Exercise 3: Case Study Analysis – Indigenous Canadian Peacemaking Circle

Purpose: To analyze how indigenous traditions were applied in a real case.

Background: (From Chapter 13)

An Indigenous community in Canada experienced ongoing conflicts related to land disputes with government agencies and neighboring communities. Traditional legal processes—lawsuits, administrative proceedings, court battles—had not resolved the deeply rooted issues and had often exacerbated tensions. Community leaders, Elders, and band council members decided to implement peacemaking circles to address the conflicts.

Peacemaking circles were convened, facilitated by Elders and respected community members. All affected parties were invited—community members, government representatives, neighboring community leaders. Circles were conducted in sacred spaces, with cultural rituals—smudging, prayers, use of the talking feather—that created spiritual atmosphere and honored Indigenous traditions. Participants shared their perspectives on the land disputes, the historical context, the impact on their communities, and their hopes for resolution. Elders guided the dialogue, emphasizing respect, empathy, and collective responsibility. Over multiple circles, participants developed agreements for shared land use, joint stewardship projects, and ongoing circles for conflict prevention and relationship maintenance.

Questions:

1. What elements of Indigenous tradition were incorporated into this process?

2. How did these elements affect the process and outcomes?

3. Why might conventional legal processes have failed where peacemaking circles succeeded?

4. How were government representatives engaged? What might they have needed to participate respectfully?

5. What lessons does this case offer for cross-cultural restorative practice?

Exercise 4: Case Study Analysis – Māori Marae Justice

Background: (From Chapter 13)

In a Māori community in New Zealand, a young person committed a crime that caused significant harm. The young person had grown up disconnected from his Māori heritage, struggling with identity, belonging, and purpose. The traditional justice system's punitive approach was not aligned with the community's values and seemed unlikely to address the underlying issues or prevent future offending.

The community chose to address the harm through a marae-based restorative justice circle. The circle was conducted on the marae, with cultural rituals and prayers opening and closing the process. Participants included the young offender, the victim, their whānau (extended families), community leaders, and a restorative justice facilitator trained in Māori protocols. During the circle, participants shared their experiences of the crime and its impact. The victim described the harm suffered; the young person spoke of his disconnection from culture and community; whānau members shared their grief and their hope. The group collaboratively developed agreements: restitution to the victim, cultural education for the young person (including regular participation in marae activities and learning te reo Māori), and community service. Whānau members committed to supporting the young person's cultural reconnection and holding him accountable for completing his agreements.

Questions:

1. How did the marae setting and cultural rituals contribute to the process?

2. What was the significance of including whānau (extended family)?

3. How did the agreement address the underlying issue of cultural disconnection?

4. What might this case teach about the relationship between cultural identity and offending?

5. How could this model be adapted (not appropriated) in other cultural contexts?

Exercise 5: Case Study Analysis – Ubuntu-Inspired Circle in South Africa

Background: (From Chapter 13)

A South African community faced a series of thefts that eroded trust and safety among residents. The formal justice system's approach—arrest, prosecution, imprisonment—had not addressed the community's broader needs for healing and had not prevented continued offending. Community members, frustrated with the system's inadequacy, decided to implement restorative justice circles inspired by Ubuntu philosophy.

Ubuntu circles were convened, facilitated by community leaders respected for their wisdom and integrity. Circles included offenders, victims, and community members. Circles began with acknowledgment of the harm and its impact. Victims shared their experiences—not only the material loss but the fear, the anger, the erosion of trust. Offenders spoke of their circumstances—poverty, unemployment, family pressures—that had led to their actions. Community members discussed the broader impact of the thefts on community cohesion and safety. They also acknowledged community failures—lack of opportunities for youth, inadequate support for struggling families—that contributed to the conditions in which offending occurred. Together, participants developed agreements: restitution where possible, community service projects that would benefit the whole community, and ongoing circles to address underlying issues and monitor progress. The circles continued as regular community gatherings, providing ongoing forum for addressing concerns, supporting vulnerable members, and maintaining the relationships that prevent crime.

Questions:

1. How does this case reflect Ubuntu philosophy ("a person is a person through persons")?

2. What was significant about community members acknowledging their own failures?

3. How did the process address both individual and systemic dimensions of harm?

4. Why did the circles continue as regular community gatherings? What purpose did this serve?

5. What might this case teach about community ownership of restorative justice?

Exercise 6: Cultural Humility Self-Assessment

Purpose: To assess your own cultural humility and identify areas for growth.

Instructions: Rate yourself on each statement from 1 (rarely true) to 5 (almost always true).

Statement	Rating (1-5)
I am aware of my own cultural background and how it shapes my views	
I recognize that my way of seeing things is not the only way	

Statement	Rating (1-5)
I approach cultural differences with curiosity, not judgment	
I ask questions when I don't understand someone's cultural perspective	
I am willing to be corrected when I make cultural mistakes	
I learn about the cultural backgrounds of people I work with	
I adapt my facilitation style to different cultural contexts	
I avoid assuming that restorative practices developed in one context will work in another	
I seek out and respect cultural leaders and elders	

Statement	Rating (1-5)
I give credit to the cultural sources of restorative practices	
I am aware of power dynamics related to culture in my work	
I actively work to ensure marginalized cultural voices are heard	

Total: _____ / 60

My greatest strengths:

Areas for growth:

One thing I will do to increase my cultural humility:

Circle Practice: "A Cultural Tradition That Shaped Me"

Purpose: To share and learn from the diverse cultural traditions represented in the group.

Time: 60–75 minutes

Materials: Talking piece, comfortable seating

Opening (5 minutes):

- Welcome participants.
- Remind of confidentiality.
- Introduce the prompt: "Share a cultural tradition from your background that has shaped how you understand community, conflict, or justice. This could be a story, a practice, a value, or a teaching passed down in your family or community."

Check-In Round (10 minutes):

- Pass the talking piece. Each person shares their name and one word about how they're arriving.

Sharing Round (30–40 minutes):

- Pass the talking piece. Each person who wishes responds to the prompt.
- Allow silence between speakers.
- No cross-talk or response.

Reflection Round (10–15 minutes):

- Pass the talking piece. Each person shares: "What did I learn from hearing about these diverse traditions? What connections do I see?"

Closing (5 minutes):

- Thank participants.
- Celebrate the richness of traditions represented.
- Close with a moment of silence.

Practical Assignment: Cultural Learning Project

Purpose: To deepen understanding of a specific cultural approach to restorative justice.

Instructions:

1. Choose a cultural tradition **not your own** that has restorative elements. Examples:
    - First Nations peacemaking circles
    - Māori family group conferencing
    - Ubuntu-inspired processes
    - Japanese *chōtei* or apology practices
    - Middle Eastern *sulha* (traditional conflict resolution)
    - Latin American indigenous practices
    - Asian communal approaches
2. Research this tradition using respectful sources:

- Seek out materials created by people from that culture
- If possible, speak with someone from that cultural community (with appropriate compensation for their time and expertise)
- Learn about the cultural context, values, and practices

3. Write a 3-4 page paper addressing:
    - Key elements of the tradition
    - Cultural values that underlie it
    - How it addresses harm and restoration
    - What restorative justice practitioners can learn from it
    - How to learn from this tradition respectfully, without appropriation
4. Include a reflection on:
    - What you learned about your own cultural assumptions
    - How you will apply this learning to your practice
    - How you will ensure your learning is respectful and reciprocal

---

Facilitator Notes for Chapter 13

Before the Session:

1. **Read Chapter 13 thoroughly.** This chapter addresses complex issues of culture, power, and appropriation. Be prepared for nuanced discussion.

2. **Examine your own cultural assumptions.** Before facilitating, reflect on your own cultural background and how it shapes your view of restorative justice.
3. **Prepare for diverse perspectives.** Participants may come from various cultural backgrounds. Create space for all voices, especially those from marginalized cultures.
4. **Gather resources.** Have information about indigenous restorative traditions from reputable, culturally respectful sources—ideally created by indigenous authors.
5. **Be mindful of appropriation.** Avoid "teaching" indigenous traditions unless you are from that culture. Instead, create space for indigenous participants to share, or use materials created by indigenous authors.

Session Outline (3–3.5 hours):

Segment	Time	Activity
Opening	10 min	Welcome, check-in, review objectives
Key Concepts	20 min	Present universality, indigenous traditions, cultural imperialism
Cultural Sensitivity Exercise	20 min	Individual work on cultural values

Segment	Time	Activity
Reflection Questions	15 min	Small group discussion on avoiding cultural imperialism
Indigenous Traditions Comparison	20 min	Small groups complete comparison table
Break	10 min	
Case Study 1: Indigenous Canadian	15 min	Analyze peacemaking circle case
Case Study 2: Māori	15 min	Analyze marae justice case
Case Study 3: Ubuntu	15 min	Analyze Ubuntu case
Cultural Humility Self-Assessment	10 min	Individual assessment

Segment	Time	Activity
Circle Practice	25 min	"A Cultural Tradition That Shaped Me"
Closing & Assignment	5 min	Review cultural learning project

Key Teaching Points:

1. **Restorative justice is not a Western invention.** It draws on ancient indigenous wisdom. Acknowledge and honor these origins.
2. **Cultural humility is essential.** You cannot know everything about another culture. Approach with openness, respect, and willingness to learn and be corrected.
3. **Avoid appropriation.** Do not extract practices from their cultural context. Learn from, partner with, and credit indigenous communities.
4. **Universal principles, culturally particular expressions.** The core restorative principles are universal, but their expression must be adapted to each cultural context.
5. **Power matters.** Restorative justice has often been exported from Western to non-Western contexts. Be aware of power dynamics and work for genuine partnership, not neocolonialism.

Common Questions:

- **Q: "How can I learn about indigenous restorative practices without appropriating them?"**
A: Seek out indigenous-led organizations, read works by indigenous authors, attend trainings led by indigenous practitioners. Offer compensation for their time and expertise. Give credit. Support indigenous justice initiatives.
- **Q: "What if I'm from the dominant culture and most participants are from marginalized cultures?"**
A: Be aware of power dynamics. Create space for marginalized voices to lead. Consider co-facilitation with someone from that culture. Be humble and open to learning.
- **Q: "How do I handle cultural practices that conflict with restorative principles?"**
A: This is complex. Universal human rights must be respected. But be cautious about imposing your cultural judgments. Seek to understand first. Dialogue, don't dictate.
- **Q: "Can restorative justice work in cultures very different from where it developed?"**
A: Yes, because restorative principles address universal human needs. But it must be adapted to local context, with local leadership.
- **Q: "What if I make a cultural mistake?"**
A: Acknowledge it, apologize, and learn. Don't be defensive. Ask for guidance on how to do better.

After the Session:

- Follow up with anyone who shared vulnerably about their cultural experiences.
- Collect cultural learning projects if assigned.

- Prepare for Chapter 14 on building and sustaining restorative communities.

Personal Journal: Chapter 13

Date: ______________

The most important thing I learned about cultural perspectives on restorative justice:

A cultural value from my background that shapes my view of justice:

A tradition from another culture that I want to learn more about respectfully:

How I will practice cultural humility in my restorative work:

____

____

A question I'm still holding about cultural appropriation:

____

____

____

Key Terms Glossary for Chapter 13

Term	Definition
Cultural Imperialism	Imposing one's own cultural assumptions and practices on another culture
Cultural Appropriation	Taking cultural practices from another culture without understanding, permission, or reciprocity

Term	Definition
Cultural Humility	Approach of openness, respect, and willingness to learn from and be corrected by other cultures
Cultural Sensitivity	Awareness of and respect for cultural differences
Inculturation	Process by which universal principles are embodied in particular cultures
Whakawhanaungatanga	Māori concept of building and maintaining relationships; making kin
Whakapapa	Māori genealogy connecting all things
Ubuntu	African philosophy: "A person is a person through persons"
Marae	Māori sacred meeting ground, center of community life
Chōtei	Japanese mediation practice

Term	Definition
Imago Dei	Latin for "image of God"; all humans bear God's image
Fusion of Horizons	Gadamer's concept of understanding across cultural difference through dialogue

"*The book of Revelation presents a vision of the new creation that is breathtaking in its diversity: 'a great multitude that no one could count, from every nation, tribe, people and language, standing before the throne' (Revelation 7:9). This vision challenges any understanding of unity that requires uniformity, any conception of truth that denies cultural particularity, any practice of justice that ignores local context.*" — Dr. Maxwell Shimba

CHAPTER 14

Building and Sustaining Restorative Communities

Learning Objectives

By completing this chapter, you will be able to:

- **Understand the foundations** of a restorative community
- **Develop a comprehensive sustainability plan** for restorative initiatives
- **Design leadership development pathways** to ensure continuity
- **Create training pipelines** that build restorative capacity across generations

- **Establish evaluation metrics** to measure and improve restorative practices
- **Integrate restorative principles** into community institutions and culture
- **Foster community ownership** that ensures longevity beyond individual leaders
- **Design a long-term vision** for restorative community transformation

---

Key Concepts from Chapter 14

1. The Vision of a Restorative Community

The prophet Jeremiah, writing to exiles in Babylon, delivered a surprising message: "Build houses and settle down; plant gardens and eat what they produce... Seek the peace and prosperity of the city to which I have carried you into exile" (Jeremiah 29:5-7). Even in exile, even under conditions not of their choosing, the people were called to build, to plant, to seek the welfare of the community.

A restorative community is not a utopia where harm never occurs. It is a community that has built the capacity to address harm constructively when it occurs, to resolve conflict in ways that heal rather than wound, to repair relationships when they are damaged. It is a community that has planted the seeds of restorative practices and tends them faithfully.

2. The Four Foundations of a Restorative Community

Foundation	Description	Key Elements
Shared Vision and Values	Explicitly articulated, collectively owned, intentionally cultivated	Covenant development; values clarification; regular renewal
Community Engagement	Active participation of all members	Inclusive structures; outreach to marginalized; partnerships
Education and Awareness	Forming restorative citizens	Community-wide education; school integration; public awareness
Restorative Practices	Embedded in daily life	Regular circles; routine conflict resolution; integrated into meetings

3. The Covenant as Foundational Vision

The biblical concept of covenant provides the deepest foundation for restorative community. Covenant is not merely a contract—an exchange of promises conditioned on mutual performance—but a solemn commitment to faithful relationship that endures through changing circumstances, failures, and renewal.

Core Values of a Restorative Community:

Value	Meaning
Empathy	Capacity to understand and share others' feelings
Respect	Recognition of inherent dignity of every person
Accountability	Willingness to take responsibility for actions and impact
Inclusivity	Ensuring all voices are heard and valued
Repair	Commitment to make things right when harm occurs
Reintegration	Welcoming back those who have made amends

4. The Restorative Pyramid in Community Context

text
[Tier 3: Intensive Intervention]
(Specialized circles for serious harm,
re-entry support, ongoing healing)
[Tier 2: Targeted Intervention]
(Conflict resolution circles, support
circles for those facing challenges)
[Tier 1: Universal Prevention]
(Regular community-building circles,
restorative language and practices
integrated into daily life)

5. Elements of Sustainability

Element	Description
Consistent Implementation	Regular rhythms of restorative practice (daily, weekly, annual)
Training and Development	Ongoing capacity building at all levels

Element	Description
Resource Allocation	Dedicated funding, facilities, materials, personnel
Leadership Development	Pathways for new leaders to emerge
Evaluation and Adaptation	Regular assessment and continuous improvement
Institutional Support	Policies, partnerships, and systems that embed restorative practices
Community Ownership	Practices owned by community, not dependent on individuals

6. Leadership Development Pipeline

text
[Master Facilitator/Trainer]
↑
[Advanced Facilitator]
↑
[Experienced Facilitator]

↑
[Facilitator]
↑
[Co-Facilitator]
↑
[Trained Community Member]
↑
[Circle Participant]

7. Training Pipeline

Level	Audience	Content	Frequency
Awareness	All community members	Restorative principles, values, language	Ongoing
Participation	Circle participants	Circle process, roles, expectations	As needed
Basic Facilitation	New facilitators	Skills, process, ethics	Annual

Level	Audience	Content	Frequency
Advanced Facilitation	Experienced facilitators	Complex cases, trauma-informed practice	Annual
Train-the-Trainer	Master facilitators	Facilitation of training, mentoring	Biennial

8. Evaluation Metrics

Category	Metrics
Process	Number of circles; participant demographics; referral sources; completion rates
Satisfaction	Participant surveys; facilitator reflections; stakeholder feedback
Outcomes	Agreement completion; recidivism rates; conflict recurrence; relationship quality

Category	Metrics
Commu-nity Impact	School climate; workplace culture; neighborhood cohesion; trust measures
Sustaina-bility	Leadership pipeline; funding stability; policy integration; community ownership

9. Restorative Cycles in Community Building

Biological Process	Community Parallel
Genetic Blueprint	Shared vision and values guide development
Cell Communication	Community engagement enables coordination
Neural Plasticity	Education and awareness shape community "brain"
Circadian Rhythms	Consistent implementation creates restorative rhythms

Biological Process	Community Parallel
Stem Cell Differentiation	Leadership development produces specialized leaders
Homeostasis	Evaluation and adaptation maintain community health

Sustainability Plan Template

Purpose: To develop a comprehensive sustainability plan for restorative justice initiatives in a community.

Instructions: Complete each section with specific, actionable strategies for your context.

COMMUNITY CONTEXT

Community Name/Location: ____________________________________

Community Type: ☐ Neighborhood ☐ Town/City ☐ Faith Community ☐ School District ☐ Other: ____________

Current restorative initiatives (if any):

Key strengths to build on:

Key challenges to address:

SECTION 1: LEADERSHIP DEVELOPMENT

1.1 Leadership Pathway

Design a clear pathway for leadership development in your community:

Level	Role	Qualifications	Responsibilities	Support Provided
Level 1	Circle Participant			
Level 2	Trained Community Member			
Level 3	Co-Facilitator			
Level 4	Facilitator			
Level 5	Advanced Facilitator			
Level 6	Master Facilitator/Trainer			

1.2 Leadership Identification

How will you identify potential leaders at each level?

1.3 Mentoring Structure

How will experienced leaders mentor emerging leaders?

1.4 Succession Planning

How will you ensure leadership continuity when current leaders step down?

1.5 Diversity and Inclusion

How will you ensure leadership reflects the diversity of your community?

1.6 Leadership Support

What support will leaders receive? (supervision, peer consultation, self-care resources)

1.7 Recognition and Celebration

How will you recognize and celebrate leaders' contributions?

SECTION 2: TRAINING PIPELINE

2.1 Training Levels

Level	Au-di-ence	Learning Ob-jec-tives	For mat	Du-ra-tion	Fre-quency	Fa-cil-ita-tors
Awareness						
Partic-ipation						
Basic Facili-tation						
Ad-vanced Facili-tation						
Train-the-Trainer						

2.2 Training Curriculum Outline

Awareness Level:

Topics: ____

Materials needed: ____

Participation Level:

Topics: ____

Materials needed: ____

Basic Facilitation:

Topics: ____

Materials needed: ____

Advanced Facilitation:

Topics: ____

Materials needed: ____

Train-the-Trainer:

Topics: ____

Materials needed: ____

2.3 Trainer Development

How will you develop and support trainers?

2.4 Training Schedule

Training	Fre-quency	Capacity (par-tici-pants/year)	Lo-cat-ion	Lead Trainer
Aware-ness				
Participa-tion				
Basic Fa-cilitation				
Advanced Facilita-tion				

Training	Fre-quency	Capacity (par-tici-pants/year)	Lo-cat-ion	Lead Trainer
Train-the-Trainer				

2.5 Training Materials

What training materials will you develop or acquire?

2.6 Training Evaluation

How will you evaluate training effectiveness?

2.7 Continuing Education

What ongoing learning opportunities will be available for trained facilitators?

SECTION 3: EVALUATION METRICS

3.1 Process Metrics

Metric	Data Source	Collection Frequency	Target	Responsible Party
Number of circles conducted				
Number of participants				
Participant demographics				
Referral sources				

Metric	Data Source	Collection Frequency	Target	Responsible Party
Circle types (community-building, conflict, re-entry)				
Completion rates				
Facilitator hours				

3.2 Satisfaction Metrics

Metric	Data Source	Collection Frequency	Target	Responsible Party
Participant satisfaction (victims)				

Metric	Data Source	Collection Frequency	Target	Responsible Party
Participant satisfaction (offenders)				
Participant satisfaction (community)				
Facilitator satisfaction				
Stakeholder satisfaction (referral sources)				
Perceptions of fairness				

Metric	Data Source	Collection Frequency	Target	Responsible Party
Willingness to recommend				

3.3 Outcome Metrics

Metric	Data Source	Collection Frequency	Target	Responsible Party
Agreement completion rate				
Restitution completion				
Community service completion				

Metric	Data Source	Collection Frequency	Target	Responsible Party
Recidivism (if applicable)				
Conflict recurrence				
Relationship improvement (self-reported)				
Emotional healing (victim)				
Behavioral change (offender)				

3.4 Community Impact Metrics

Metric	Data Source	Collection Frequency	Base-line	Tar-get
School climate (if applicable)				
Workplace culture (if applicable)				
Neighborhood cohesion				
Trust in community institutions				
Sense of belonging				
Collective efficacy				

Metric	Data Source	Collection Frequency	Baseline	Target
Crime rates (relevant offenses)				

Use of restorative language

3.5 Sustainability Metrics

Metric	Data Source	Collection Frequency	Target	Responsible Party
Number of active facilitators				
Facilitator retention rate				

Metric	Data Source	Collection Frequency	Target	Responsible Party
New facilitators trained per year				
Leadership pipeline diversity				
Funding stability				
Policy integration				
Partnership strength				
Community ownership (surveys)				

3.6 Evaluation Process

How will data be collected?

How will data be analyzed and reported?

How will findings be used for continuous improvement?

How will findings be shared with the community?

3.7 Evaluation Schedule

Evaluation Activity	Frequency	Responsible Party

SECTION 4: RESOURCE ALLOCATION

4.1 Budget Categories

Category	Year 1	Year 2	Year 3	Year 4	Year 5
Coordinator/Staff					
Facilitator Stipends					
Training (materials, trainers, venue)					

Category	Year 1	Year 2	Year 3	Year 4	Year 5
Evaluation					
Facilities/ Space					
Outreach/Marketing					
Technology					
Supplies					
Community Events					
TOTAL					

4.2 Funding Sources

Source	Year 1	Year 2	Year 3	Year 4	Year 5	Status (secured/pending)
Grants						
Government funding						
Institutional partners						
Donations						
Fee-for-						

Source	Year 1	Year 2	Year 3	Year 4	Year 5	Status (secured/pending)
service						
In-kind contributions						
TOTAL						

4.3 In-Kind Resources

Resource	Source	Estimated Value
Volunteer facilitators		
Donated space		

Resource	Source	Estimated Value
Pro bono services		
Materials		

Other:

4.4 Resource Development Plan

What strategies will you use to develop and sustain resources?

SECTION 5: PARTNERSHIPS AND INSTITUTIONAL SUPPORT

5.1 Key Partners

Partner	Role	Resources They Provide	MOUs Needed?

5.2 Policy Integration

What policies need to be developed or revised to embed restorative practices?

Policy Area	Current Status	Needed Changes	Responsible Party	Timeline

5.3 Institutional Champions

Who are the champions within key institutions? How will you cultivate them?

5.4 Partnership Agreements

What formal agreements (MOUs) are needed with partners?

SECTION 6: COMMUNICATION AND OUTREACH

6.1 Communication Goals

6.2 Target Audiences

Audience	Key Messages	Communication Channels	Frequency
Community members			
Potential participants			
Potential facilitators			
Partners			
Funders			

Audience	Key Messages	Communication Channels	Frequency
Media			

6.3 Success Story Collection

How will you collect and share success stories?

6.4 Public Awareness Campaigns

What campaigns will you conduct to build awareness and support?

SECTION 7: TIMELINE

Activity	Year 1	Year 2	Year 3	Year 4	Year 5
Foundation Building					
Leadership identification					
Facilitator training					
Partner MOUs					
Policy development					
Implementation					
Regular circles begin					

Activity	Year 1	Year 2	Year 3	Year 4	Year 5
Community-building circles					
Conflict resolution circles					
Capacity Building					
Advanced facilitator training					
Train-the-trainer					
Peer learning groups					
Evaluation & Improvement					

Activity	Year 1	Year 2	Year 3	Year 4	Year 5
Baseline data collection					
Annual evaluation					
Program adjustments					
Expansion					
New neighborhoods/areas					
New partner engagement					
Policy expansion					

Practical Assignment: Design a 5-Year Restorative Community Vision

Purpose: To synthesize learning from this chapter by creating a comprehensive vision for building a restorative community over five years.

Instructions: Using the template below, design a detailed 5-year vision for a restorative community. This can be for your actual community or a hypothetical one. Be specific, ambitious, and practical.

5-YEAR RESTORATIVE COMMUNITY VISION

Community Name: ____________________________________

Date: ____________________________________

Vision Developer: ____________________________________

PART 1: VISION STATEMENT

In 5 years, our community will be...

(Write a compelling vision of what your community will look like, feel like, and be known for. Include restorative values, practices, and outcomes.)

PART 2: CORE VALUES

The values that will guide our restorative community:

1.
2.
3.
4.
5.

PART 3: 5-YEAR GOALS

Goal 1: Restorative Practices Embedded in Daily Life

Target	Year 1	Year 2	Year 3	Year 4	Year 5
Number of community-building circles					
Number of conflict resolution circles					
Percentage of schools with restorative practices					
Percentage of workplaces with restorative options					

Target	Year 1	Year 2	Year 3	Year 4	Year 5
Restorative language commonly used					

Goal 2: Trained Facilitators and Leaders

Target	Year 1	Year 2	Year 3	Year 4	Year 5
Number of trained facilitators					
Number of advanced facilitators					
Number of master facilitators/trainers					

Target	Year 1	Year 2	Year 3	Year 4	Year 5
Facilitator retention rate					
Leadership diversity (demographics)					

Goal 3: Community Engagement and Ownership

Target	Year 1	Year 2	Year 3	Year 4	Year 5
Percentage of community aware of restorative justice					
Percentage who have participated in a circle					

Target	Year 1	Year 2	Year 3	Year 4	Year 5
Number of active community partners					
Community satisfaction with restorative processes					
Sense of community belonging (survey)					

Goal 4: Institutional Integration

Target	Year 1	Year 2	Year 3	Year 4	Year 5
Schools with restorative policies					

Target	Year 1	Year 2	Year 3	Year 4	Year 5
Law enforcement partnerships					
Social service integration					
Government recognition/support					
Restorative justice in local codes/policies					

Goal 5: Measurable Outcomes

Target	Year 1	Year 2	Year 3	Year 4	Year 5
Agreement completion rate					
Recidivism reduction (if applicable)					
Conflict recurrence rate					
Victim satisfaction					
Offender accountability (self-reported)					

Goal 6: Sustainability

Target	Year 1	Year 2	Year 3	Year 4	Year 5
Annual budget secured					
Funding sources diversified					
New facilitators trained annually					
Leadership succession plan in place					
Community ownership (not dependent on individuals)					

PART 4: KEY STRATEGIES

For each goal, describe the key strategies you will use to achieve it.

Goal 1: Restorative Practices Embedded

Strategies:

Goal 2: Trained Facilitators and Leaders

Strategies:

Goal 3: Community Engagement

Strategies:

Goal 4: Institutional Integration

Strategies:

Goal 5: Measurable Outcomes

Strategies:

Goal 6: Sustainability

Strategies:

____

____

____

PART 5: KEY MILESTONES BY YEAR

Year 1 Milestones:

1. ______________________________________
2. ______________________________________
3. ______________________________________
4. ______________________________________
5. ______________________________________

Year 2 Milestones:

1. ______________________________________
2. ______________________________________
3. ______________________________________
4. ______________________________________
5. ______________________________________

Year 3 Milestones:

1. ______________________________________
2. ______________________________________
3. ______________________________________
4. ______________________________________
5. ______________________________________

Year 4 Milestones:

1. ______________________________________

2. ....
3. ....
4. ....
5. ....

Year 5 Milestones:

1. ....
2. ....
3. ....
4. ....
5. ....

PART 6: RESOURCE REQUIREMENTS

Personnel Needed:

Role	Year 1	Year 2	Year 3	Year 4	Year 5

Annual Budget Estimate:

Category	Year 1	Year 2	Year 3	Year 4	Year 5
Personnel					

Category	Year 1	Year 2	Year 3	Year 4	Year 5
Training					
Operations					
Evaluation					
Outreach					
TOTAL					

Potential Funding Sources:

1. ______________________________
2. ______________________________
3. ______________________________
4. ______________________________
5. ______________________________

PART 7: PARTNERSHIPS NEEDED

Partner	Role	Current Relationship	Actions Needed

PART 8: POTENTIAL CHALLENGES AND MITIGATIONS

Challenge	Likelihood (H/M/L)	Impact (H/M/L)	Mitigation Strategy

PART 9: SUCCESS LOOKS LIKE

In 5 years, how will you know you've succeeded? Describe what success looks like in vivid detail.

PART 10: PERSONAL COMMITMENT

What is my personal role in making this vision a reality?

What am I willing to commit?

What support do I need?

Reflection Questions on 5-Year Vision

1. What part of this vision excites you most?

2. What part feels most challenging?

3. Who needs to be involved for this vision to become reality?

4. What is the first step you could take toward this vision?

5. How will you sustain hope and momentum over five years?

6. What lessons do indigenous justice systems offer for building sustainable restorative communities? Consider: intergenerational transmission, role of elders, community ownership, connection to land and culture, holistic approaches.

Circle Practice: "My Hope for Our Community"

Purpose: To share hopes and build collective vision for restorative community.

Time: 45–60 minutes

Materials: Talking piece, comfortable seating

Opening (5 minutes):

- Welcome participants.
- Remind of confidentiality.

- Introduce the prompt: "Share your hope for our community (or a community you care about) in 5 years. What would a restorative community look like, feel like, and be known for?"

Check-In Round (10 minutes):

- Pass the talking piece. Each person shares their name and one word about how they're arriving.

Sharing Round (20–30 minutes):

- Pass the talking piece. Each person who wishes responds to the prompt.
- Allow silence between speakers.
- No cross-talk or response.

Reflection Round (10 minutes):

- Pass the talking piece. Each person shares: "What did I hear in these hopes? What common themes emerged? What will it take to make these hopes real?"

Closing (5 minutes):

- Thank participants.
- Affirm the power of shared vision.
- Close with a moment of silence.

Facilitator Notes for Chapter 14

Before the Session:

1. **Read Chapter 14 thoroughly.** This chapter synthesizes everything that has come before and looks toward the future. Understand the four foundations and elements of sustainability.
2. **Prepare templates.** Have copies of the Sustainability Plan Template and 5-Year Vision Template for all participants.
3. **Think long-term.** Encourage participants to think beyond immediate implementation to lasting transformation.
4. **Gather examples.** If possible, bring examples of communities that have sustained restorative practices over time.

Session Outline (3.5–4 hours):

Segment	Time	Activity
Opening	10 min	Welcome, check-in, review objectives
Key Concepts	20 min	Present four foundations, sustainability elements
Sustainability Plan Introduction	15 min	Review template sections

Segment	Time	Activity
Leadership Development	20 min	Small group work on leadership pipeline
Training Pipeline	20 min	Small group work on training levels
Break	10 min	
Evaluation Metrics	20 min	Small group work on metrics
Resource Allocation	15 min	Discuss funding and resources
5-Year Vision Introduction	15 min	Review vision template
Vision Development	40 min	Individual work on 5-year vision

Segment	Time	Activity
Vision Sharing	20 min	Partners share visions; large group themes
Circle Practice	20 min	"My Hope for Our Community"
Closing & Assignment	5 min	Complete 5-year vision as assignment

Key Teaching Points:

1. **Sustainability requires intention.** Restorative practices will not sustain themselves. They require ongoing investment, training, and leadership development.
2. **Community ownership is essential.** Practices owned by the community will outlast any individual leader or program.
3. **Multiple levels of intervention.** The pyramid model (universal, targeted, intensive) applies to communities as well as schools.
4. **Evaluation is for learning, not just accountability.** Use data to improve, not just to prove.
5. **Vision sustains hope.** A compelling long-term vision keeps people engaged through challenges.

Common Questions:

- **Q: "How do we sustain restorative practices when funding runs out?"**
  A: Diversify funding sources. Build in-kind contributions. Demonstrate value to secure ongoing support. Most importantly, build community ownership so practices continue even without formal funding.
- **Q: "What if key leaders leave?"**
  A: Succession planning is essential. Develop leadership pipelines so new leaders are ready. Document processes so institutional knowledge isn't lost.
- **Q: "How do we know if we're making a difference?"**
  A: Use the evaluation metrics. Track both short-term outcomes (satisfaction, agreement completion) and long-term impact (community cohesion, reduced conflict).
- **Q: "How long does it take to build a restorative community?"**
  A: Years, not months. The 5-year vision is realistic. Some communities take a generation. Patience and persistence are essential.
- **Q: "What if the community doesn't want restorative justice?"**
  A: Start where they are. Build relationships. Demonstrate value through small successes. Let community ownership emerge organically.

After the Session:

- Collect 5-year visions for feedback.
- Connect participants with resources for long-term planning.
- Prepare for Chapter 15 on future directions.

Personal Journal: Chapter 14

Date: _______________

The most important thing I learned about sustainability:

A leadership quality I want to develop:

A metric that matters most to me:

One thing I will do to build sustainability in my context:

My hope for my community in 5 years:

A question I'm still holding about sustainability:

Key Terms Glossary for Chapter 14

Term	Definition
Restorative Community	A community with capacity to address harm constructively, resolve conflict healingly, and repair relationships
Covenant	Solemn commitment to faithful relationship; foundation for shared vision

Term	Definition
Pyramid Model	Three tiers: universal prevention, targeted intervention, intensive response
Sustainability	Capacity to maintain restorative practices over time
Leadership Pipeline	Pathway for developing new leaders at all levels
Training Pipeline	System for building restorative capacity across the community
Evaluation Metrics	Measures to assess process, satisfaction, outcomes, and impact
Community Ownership	Practices owned and sustained by community, not dependent on individuals
Succession Planning	Preparing for leadership transitions

Term	Definition
Collective Efficacy	Shared belief that community can solve problems together
Social Capital	Networks of relationships, trust, and reciprocity

"A restorative community is not a utopia where harm never occurs. It is a community that has built the capacity to address harm constructively when it occurs, to resolve conflict in ways that heal rather than wound, to repair relationships when they are damaged." — Dr. Maxwell Shimba

CHAPTER 15

Future Directions for Restorative Justice Circles

Learning Objectives

By completing this chapter, you will be able to:

- **Identify emerging trends** shaping the future of restorative justice
- **Explore innovative applications** of restorative principles in new contexts
- **Brainstorm creative ways** technology, policy, and education can expand restorative justice
- **Articulate a personal vision** for the future of restorative justice

- **Reflect on your own transformation** through this study
- **Commit to ongoing growth** and contribution to the restorative justice movement
- **Synthesize learning** from all previous chapters

Key Concepts from Chapter 15

1. The Ever-Expanding Horizon of Restoration

The prophet Isaiah envisioned a day when God would "do a new thing" (Isaiah 43:19)—a reality breaking forth, demanding attention, inviting participation. The restorative justice movement stands at such a moment. What began in the 1970s as small-scale experiments has grown into a global movement. Yet this growth is not an ending but a beginning.

2. Emerging Trends

Trend	Description	Opportunities	Challenges
Technology Integration	Virtual circles; online training; digital documentation	Accessibility; reaching remote partici-	Digital divide; loss of embodied presence; security concerns

Trend	Description	Opportunities	Challenges
		pants; hybrid models	
Expanding Applications	Environmental justice; healthcare; corporate governance	Addressing new types of harm; reaching new populations	Adapting principles to new contexts; ensuring fidelity
Intersectionality	Attending to multiple identities (race, gender, class, ability)	More inclusive practice; addressing systemic harm	Complexity; need for specialized knowledge
Research and	Building evidence base; outcome measurement	Credibility; funding; continuous	Funding for research; methodological challenges

Trend	Description	Opportunities	Challenges
Evaluation		improvement	
Policy Integration	Embedding restorative justice in legal and institutional frameworks	Sustainability; systemic impact	Co-optation; bureaucratization
Global Expansion	Adaptation in diverse cultural contexts	Cross-cultural learning; global movement	Cultural imperialism; appropriation

3. Technology Integration

Technology	Applications	Considerations
Video Conferencing	Virtual circles; remote participation	Security; accessibility; "Zoom fatigue"

Technology	Applications	Considerations
Online Training Platforms	Facilitator training; continuing education	Engagement; skill practice
Digital Documentation	Agreements; follow-up tracking	Confidentiality; accessibility
Mobile Apps	Preparation resources; grounding tools	Equity of access; data security
Hybrid Models	Some in-person, some virtual	Equity; facilitator skill

Theological Reflection: The incarnation affirms embodied presence, yet the Spirit transcends physical boundaries. Virtual circles can mediate presence, facilitate dialogue, enable healing—not as replacements but as extensions.

4. Expanding Applications

Domain	Applications
Environmental Justice	Addressing pollution, resource conflicts, climate impacts; involving corporate and governmental actors; ecological restoration as reparation
Healthcare	Medical errors; adverse events; patient-provider conflicts; end-of-life decisions
Corporate Governance	Addressing fraud, discrimination, human rights abuses; transforming organizational culture
Transitional Justice	Truth commissions; post-conflict reconciliation; addressing historical injustice
Online Communities	Addressing cyberbullying, harassment, conflict in digital spaces

5. Intersectionality and Inclusivity

Dimension	Considerations
Race	Addressing racial harm; systemic racism; culturally specific practices
Gender	Sexual harm; domestic violence; gender-based oppression
Class	Economic justice; poverty as context for offending
Ability	Accessibility; accommodations; disability justice
LGBTQ+	Addressing harm related to sexual orientation and gender identity

6. Research and Evaluation Priorities

Area	Questions
Effectiveness	What works, for whom, under what conditions?

Area	Questions
Mechanisms	How does restorative justice produce change?
Implementation	What factors support or impede successful implementation?
Adaptation	How can restorative justice be adapted to new contexts while maintaining fidelity?
Cost-Benefit	What are the economic impacts of restorative justice?
Long-term Outcomes	What are the lasting effects on individuals and communities?

7. Policy Integration

Level	Opportunities
Local	Municipal ordinances; school district policies; police department protocols

Level	Opportunities
State/Provincial	Legislation authorizing restorative justice; funding; standards
National	Criminal code reform; federal funding; national standards
International	UN declarations; cross-border cooperation; global advocacy

8. Innovative Practices

Practice	Description
Trauma-Informed Circles	Integrating understanding of trauma into all phases
Hybrid Models	Combining restorative justice with therapy, case management, or other interventions
Youth-Led Initiatives	Young people as facilitators, trainers, and leaders

Practice	Description
Restorative Cities	Municipal commitments to restorative principles across all domains
Restorative Organizations	Embedding restorative practices in organizational culture

9. Restorative Cycles and the Future

Biological Process	Future Direction Parallel
Evolution	Adaptation to new environments and challenges
Speciation	Diversification into distinct forms for different contexts
Symbiosis	Integration with other movements and disciplines
Regeneration	Renewal and continuous adaptation

Innovation Brainstorm

Purpose: To generate creative ideas for expanding restorative justice through technology, policy, education, and other means.

Instructions: In small groups or individually, brainstorm as many ideas as possible for each category. Don't evaluate yet—just generate. After brainstorming, identify the most promising ideas.

CATEGORY 1: TECHNOLOGY INNOVATIONS

How can technology expand restorative justice?

Idea	Description	Potential Impact	Challenges
1.			
2.			
3.			
4.			

Idea	Description	Potential Impact	Challenges
5.			
6.			
7.			
8.			

Most Promising Ideas:

1. ________________
2. ________________
3. ________________

____

CATEGORY 2: POLICY INNOVATIONS

How can policy expand restorative justice at local, state, national, or international levels?

Idea	Description	Level	Potential Impact	Challenges
1.				
2.				
3.				
4.				
5.				
6.				
7.				
8.				

Most Promising Ideas:

1. ____________________
2. ____________________
3. ____________________

CATEGORY 3: EDUCATION INNOVATIONS

How can education expand restorative justice at all levels (K-12, higher education, professional, public)?

Idea	Description	Audience	Potential Impact	Challenges
1.				
2.				
3.				
4.				
5.				
6.				
7.				
8.				

Most Promising Ideas:

1. ____
2. ____
3. ____

CATEGORY 4: NEW APPLICATIONS

What new contexts or domains could benefit from restorative justice?

Domain	Potential Application	Why It Fits	Challenges
1.			
2.			
3.			
4.			
5.			
6.			

Domain	Potential Application	Why It Fits	Challenges
7.			
8.			

Most Promising New Applications:

1. ______
2. ______
3. ______

______

CATEGORY 5: RESEARCH PRIORITIES

What research would most advance restorative justice?

Research Question	Why It Matters	How It Could Be Studied
1.		
2.		
3.		

Research Question	Why It Matters	How It Could Be Studied
4.		
5.		
6.		

Top Research Priorities:

1. ______
2. ______
3. ______

CATEGORY 6: PARTNERSHIPS AND MOVEMENTS

What other movements or disciplines could restorative justice partner with?

Movement/Discipline	Potential Synergies	Collaborative Possibilities
1.		

Movement/Discipline	Potential Synergies	Collaborative Possibilities
2.		
3.		
4.		
5.		
6.		

Most Promising Partnerships:

1. ______________________________
2. ______________________________
3. ______________________________

Innovation Action Planning

Choose **one** promising idea from the brainstorm and develop it further.

Idea: ______________________________

Category: ☐ Technology ☐ Policy ☐ Education ☐ New Application ☐ Research ☐ Partnership

Description (what, how, for whom):

Why this idea matters:

First steps to explore this idea:

1. ______
2. ______
3. ______

Resources needed:

Potential partners:

Potential challenges and how to address them:

Timeline for exploration:

How I might contribute:

Final Reflection

Purpose: To synthesize your learning from this entire workbook and articulate how your understanding of justice has changed.

Instructions: Take time to reflect on each question. Write honestly and deeply. This is your personal testimony of transformation.

PART 1: MY JOURNEY THROUGH THIS WORKBOOK

1. When I began this study, my understanding of justice was:

2. The chapter that most challenged me was: Chapter _____ because:

3. The chapter that most inspired me was: Chapter _____ because:

4. A concept or practice I will carry forward:

5. A question I'm still holding:

PART 2: HOW MY UNDERSTANDING OF JUSTICE HAS CHANGED

6. Before this study, I thought justice was primarily about:

Now I understand justice as:

7. Before this study, I thought accountability meant:

Now I understand accountability as:

8. Before this study, I thought victims needed:

Now I understand victims need:

9. Before this study, I thought offenders deserved:

Now I understand offenders need:

10. Before this study, I saw community as:

Now I see community as:

PART 3: KEY INSIGHTS BY CHAPTER

Chapter	Key Insight I'm Taking Away
1: Introduction	
2: Principles	
3: History	
4: Implementation	
5: Facilitators	
6: Circle Process	
7: Case Studies	
8: Challenges	
9: Psychological Impact	
10: Schools	

Chapter	Key Insight I'm Taking Away
11: Workplace	
12: Criminal Justice	
13: Cultural Perspectives	
14: Sustainable Communities	

15: Future Directions

PART 4: PERSONAL TRANSFORMATION

11. How have I been changed by this study?

12. What personal wounds or biases have I become more aware of?

13. What strengths have I discovered in myself?

14. What fears or hesitations do I still have about restorative justice?

15. What gives me hope?

PART 5: MY COMMITMENT

16. What is my personal vision for restorative justice in my sphere of influence?

17. What role will I play in advancing restorative justice?

☐ Facilitator
☐ Advocate
☐ Educator
☐ Trainer
☐ Researcher
☐ Community builder
☐ Policy influencer
☐ Other: ______________

18. Specific commitments I make:

Commitment	Timeline	Support Needed

19. Who will support me in these commitments?

20. How will I continue learning and growing?

PART 6: MESSAGE TO MY FUTURE SELF

Write a letter to yourself to read one year from now. Include:

- What you've learned
- What you hope you'll remember
- What you hope you'll have done
- Words of encouragement

Circle Practice: "A Hope I Carry Forward"

Purpose: To share hopes and commitments as a closing ritual for this study.

Time: 60–75 minutes

Materials: Talking piece, comfortable seating, candles or other ritual objects (optional)

Opening (10 minutes):

- Welcome participants to this final circle.
- Acknowledge the journey you've taken together.
- Remind of confidentiality.
- Introduce the prompt: "Share a hope you carry forward from this study—for yourself, for your community, for restorative justice, or for the world."

Check-In Round (10 minutes):

- Pass the talking piece. Each person shares their name and one word about how they're arriving at this final circle.

Sharing Round (30–40 minutes):

- Pass the talking piece. Each person who wishes responds to the prompt.
- Allow silence between speakers.
- No cross-talk or response.

Reflection Round (10 minutes):

- Pass the talking piece. Each person shares: "What will I remember from this circle and this journey?"

Closing Ritual (5–10 minutes):

- Light a candle or use another ritual to symbolize the light of restorative justice continuing.
- Invite each person to speak one word as the talking piece passes one last time.
- Thank participants for their vulnerability, honesty, and commitment.

- Close with these words or your own:

"The restorative cycles continue to turn. The journey continues. And we are invited to walk it together. Go in peace, and may the work of restoration continue in and through you."

Practical Assignment: My Restorative Justice Vision Project

Purpose: To synthesize all learning into a personal vision project that can guide your future work.

Instructions: Choose ONE of the following options to complete as a final project.

Option A: Restorative Justice Initiative Proposal

Develop a detailed proposal for a restorative justice initiative in a context of your choice. Include:

- Needs assessment
- Vision and goals
- Target population
- Program design (circle types, referral process, etc.)
- Facilitator training plan
- Partnerships needed
- Budget and resources
- Evaluation plan
- Sustainability plan
- Timeline

Option B: Restorative Justice Training Curriculum

Design a training curriculum for a specific audience (facilitators, teachers, community members, etc.). Include:

- Learning objectives
- Module outlines
- Key content
- Activities and exercises
- Materials needed
- Evaluation methods
- Facilitator guide

Option C: Restorative Justice Policy Paper

Write a policy paper advocating for restorative justice integration in a specific system (schools, criminal justice, workplace, etc.). Include:

- Problem statement
- Evidence base
- Policy recommendations
- Implementation considerations
- Addressing counterarguments
- Call to action

Option D: Personal Restorative Justice Portfolio

Create a portfolio documenting your learning and growth. Include:

- Revised versions of key exercises from each chapter
- Your 5-Year Restorative Community Vision (from Chapter 14)
- Your innovation action plan (from this chapter)
- Your final reflection

- Any additional work you're proud of
- A personal statement of your restorative justice philosophy

Facilitator Notes for Chapter 15

Before the Session:

1. **Read Chapter 15 thoroughly.** This final chapter looks forward. Be prepared to help participants synthesize and project.
2. **Prepare for closure.** This is the final session. Create a meaningful closing experience that honors the journey.
3. **Gather innovation resources.** Have examples of innovative restorative justice programs or technologies to spark brainstorming.
4. **Prepare final circle.** This circle should be especially meaningful. Consider candles, music, or other ritual elements.

Session Outline (3–3.5 hours):

Segment	Time	Activity
Opening	10 min	Welcome, review objectives
Key Concepts	20 min	Present emerging trends and future directions

Segment	Time	Activity
Innovation Brain-storm	40 min	Small groups brainstorm all categories
Innovation Sharing	20 min	Groups share most promising ideas
Innovation Action Planning	15 min	Individual work on one idea
Break	10 min	
Final Reflection	30 min	Individual written reflection
Reflection Sharing	20 min	Partners share key insights
Closing Circle	45 min	"A Hope I Carry Forward"

Segment	Time	Activity
Final Words	5 min	Closing remarks, assignment

Key Teaching Points:

1. **The future is unwritten.** It will be shaped by those who show up, who innovate, who persist.
2. **Innovation must be grounded in principles.** New applications must maintain fidelity to restorative values.
3. **Technology is a tool, not a solution.** It can extend restorative justice but cannot replace embodied presence and relationship.
4. **Partnerships amplify impact.** Restorative justice cannot solve systemic problems alone. Partner with other movements.
5. **The journey continues.** Completion of this workbook is not an end but a beginning.

Common Questions:

- **Q: "How do I stay involved after this study ends?"**
  A: Join restorative justice networks. Find local initiatives. Start something in your context. Continue learning. Connect with others.
- **Q: "What if I'm not ready to facilitate?"**
  A: There are many roles—advocate, educator, community builder, supporter. Keep learning. Seek mentorship.

- **Q: "How do I handle setbacks?"**
  A: They will come. Remember the restorative cycles—inflammation, proliferation, remodeling. Setbacks are part of the process.
- **Q: "What gives you hope for the future of restorative justice?"**
  A: The growing movement worldwide. The creativity of practitioners. The enduring human need for healing and connection. The God who makes all things new.

After the Session:

- Celebrate completion of the workbook.
- Collect final projects if assigned.
- Provide information about next steps, networks, and resources.
- Stay connected with participants if possible.

Personal Journal: Chapter 15 and Final Reflection

Date: _______________

An innovation that excites me:

A fear I have about the future:

A hope I carry forward:

How I have changed:

What I will do next:

A blessing I would offer to others on this journey:

Key Terms Glossary for Chapter 15

Term	Definition
Emerging Trends	New developments shaping the future of restorative justice
Technology Integration	Use of digital tools to extend restorative practice
Expanding Applications	New contexts for restorative justice (environmental, healthcare, etc.)
Intersectionality	Attention to multiple identities and systems of oppression
Hybrid Models	Combining restorative justice with other interventions
Restorative Cities	Municipal commitments to restorative principles across all domains

Term	Definition
Transitional Justice	Processes for addressing historical injustice and post-conflict reconciliation
Speciation	Biological metaphor for diversification of restorative justice into distinct forms
Symbiosis	Biological metaphor for mutually beneficial partnerships with other movements

---

Closing Blessing

May the restorative cycles that sustain all life continue to turn in you and through you.

May you carry forward the wisdom of indigenous elders who preserved restorative traditions through centuries of oppression.

May you learn from the Anabaptist peacemakers who initiated the modern restorative justice movement.

May you honor the victims whose voices have been silenced and the offenders who have found accountability and transformation.

May you build communities where harm is addressed constructively, relationships are repaired, and all can flourish.

May you know that you do not walk alone—but with generations of restorative practitioners, with communities committed to healing, with the Spirit who empowers, the Son who reconciles, and the Father who restores.

Go in peace. The work of restoration continues. And you are part of it.

— Dr. Maxwell Shimba

Congratulations on completing the Restorative Justice Circles Workbook!

"The restorative cycles of creation await our participation. The God of reconciliation calls us to join the divine work of making all things new."

FINAL COVENANT STATEMENT

A Commitment to Restorative Justice

Instructions for Use

This Final Covenant Statement is designed to be completed after finishing all fifteen chapters of the *Restorative Justice Circles Workbook*. It serves as a personal and communal commitment to embody the principles and practices you have studied.

Options for Use:

- **Individual Completion:** Complete this statement privately as a personal commitment to yourself and to the restorative journey.
- **Group Ceremony:** Complete this statement together as a group, perhaps as part of the final circle practice in Chapter 15. Each person signs their own copy, and copies may be exchanged as symbols of mutual commitment.
- **Facilitated Ceremony:** A facilitator may lead a covenant ceremony, inviting each person to read their commitment aloud before signing.

Preparation for Covenant

Before signing, take time to reflect on these questions. You may wish to write your answers in your journal.

1. What has been the most significant learning from this study?

---

2. What is the greatest challenge I anticipate in living out restorative values?

---

3. What support will I need to sustain this commitment?

4. Who will hold me accountable to this covenant?

5. What hope do I carry forward?

Communal Reading

If completing this covenant in a group, read the following together before signing individually.

Leader: We have studied together the principles and practices of restorative justice. We have learned that justice is not merely about punishment but about healing, not about winning but about restoring, not about excluding but about reintegrating.

All: We have learned that harm affects victims, offenders, and communities—and that all must be part of repair.

Leader: We have learned that accountability means active responsibility, not passive suffering.

All: We have learned that reparation must be tangible, and reintegration must be real.

Leader: We have learned from indigenous elders who preserved restorative wisdom through centuries of oppression.

All: We have learned from faith traditions that testify to a God who reconciles and restores.

Leader: We have learned that the circle is sacred space where all voices are equal, all are heard, and all are honored.

All: We have learned that the restorative cycles of wounding and healing, rupture and repair, are woven into the fabric of creation.

Leader: Now we come to the moment of commitment. We do not make this covenant lightly. We make it with awareness of our own wounds, our own biases, our own limitations. We make it with hope.

All: We make it together.

Personal Covenant Statement

I, ______________________________, having studied the principles and practices of restorative justice, do hereby commit to the following:

I commit to practicing justice that heals.

I will seek not merely to assign blame or impose consequences, but to understand the full impact of harm and to support the healing of all affected parties. I will remember that victims need voice, validation, and reparation—not just the satisfaction of offenders' suffering.

I commit to practicing justice that restores.

I will pursue accountability that is active, not passive—responsibility that leads to making amends, not just enduring punishment. I will support offenders in understanding the impact of their actions and in taking concrete steps to repair harm.

I commit to practicing justice that reconciles.

I will work to rebuild relationships that have been broken by harm. I will support the reintegration of those who have made amends. I will remember that community is not whole until all its members are welcomed back.

I commit to embodying the principles of restorative justice:

Principle	My Commitment
Inclusivity	I will seek out and include all affected parties.
Voluntariness	I will honor free choice and the right to withdraw.
Respect and Equality	I will treat all with dignity and ensure all voices are heard.
Accountability	I will encourage active responsibility, not passive punishment.

Principle	My Commitment
Reparation	I will support tangible repair of harm.
Reintegration	I will welcome back those who have made amends.

I commit to ongoing growth:

- I will continue to learn about restorative justice.
- I will seek feedback on my practice.
- I will remain open to correction and new understanding.
- I will practice self-care to sustain this work.
- I will connect with others on this journey.

I commit to these specific actions in the coming year:

1. ____________________
2. ____________________

3. ______
4. ______
5. ______

______

I acknowledge that I will not do this perfectly.

There will be times when I fail to listen, when I am impatient, when I judge rather than seek to understand. There will be times when my own wounds get in the way, when my biases distort my perception, when I fall short of my commitments.

When this happens, I will:

- Acknowledge my failure
- Seek to repair any harm I have caused
- Learn from the experience
- Return to this covenant and begin again

______

______

______

I make this covenant in the presence of:

______

______

I am sustained in this work by:

I carry forward this hope:

Signatures

My Commitment:

(Signature)

(Printed Name)

(Date)

(Location)

Witnessed by:

(Signature)

(Printed Name)

(Date)

Witnessed by:

(Signature)

(Printed Name)

(Date)

Covenant Keepers

List the names of those who have made this covenant, to serve as a mutual support network.

Name	Contact	I commit to supporting them by...

Annual Renewal

This covenant is not made once but renewed each year. Return to this page annually to recommit.

First Renewal:

Date: _____________ Signature: _____________

Reflection on the past year:

Commitments for the coming year:

Second Renewal:

Date: ______________ Signature: ______________

Reflection on the past year:

Commitments for the coming year:

Third Renewal:

Date: ______________ Signature: ______________

Reflection on the past year:

Commitments for the coming year:

Closing Blessing

May the God of reconciliation walk with you.

May the Spirit of wisdom guide you.

May the restorative cycles of creation sustain you.

May the community of fellow travelers encourage you.

And may the work of restoration—in you, through you, and around you—continue and grow.

Go in peace. The journey continues.

"The restorative cycles continue to turn. The journey continues. And we are invited to walk it together." — Dr. Maxwell Shimba

---

www.ingramcontent.com/pod-product-compliance
Lightning Source LLC
LaVergne TN
LVHW052206200926
848481LV00001B/37
9798295630668